Young Jesus Chronicles

Young Jesus Chronicles

by Spencer Smith and Mark Penta

Andrews McMeel
Publishing, LLC
Kansas City • Sydney • London

10 11 12 13 14 BBG 10 9 8 7 6 5 4 3 2 1

ISBN-13: 978-0-7407-9259-5
ISBN-10: 0-7407-9259-8

Library of Congress Control Number: 2009938772

www.andrewsmcmeel.com
www.youngjesuschronicles.com

ATTENTION: SCHOOLS AND BUSINESSES

Andrews McMeel books are available at quantity discounts with bulk purchase for educational, business, or sales promotional use. For information, please write to: Special Sales Department, Andrews McMeel Publishing, LLC, 1130 Walnut Street, Kansas City, Missouri 64106.

Spencer would like to thank:
Everyone who has endured listening to him
talk about this book over the last ten years,
as if it were actually going to happen
(especially Mom, Zachary, and family).

Mark would like to thank:
Spencer, for his great sense of humor,
and Jesus, who he prays has one.

They both thank:
JoAnne, Cliff, Jessica, and Ted.

Introduction

For centuries, readers of the New Testament were left to speculate about Jesus's childhood.

Recently, archaeologists made a startling discovery, unearthing what theologians and historians alike have hailed as "the definitive account of the life and times of a boy named Jesus."

Due to the significance of this unprecedented finding, the Vatican called upon the world's foremost experts to decipher these time-ravaged documents . . .

0-VI A.D.

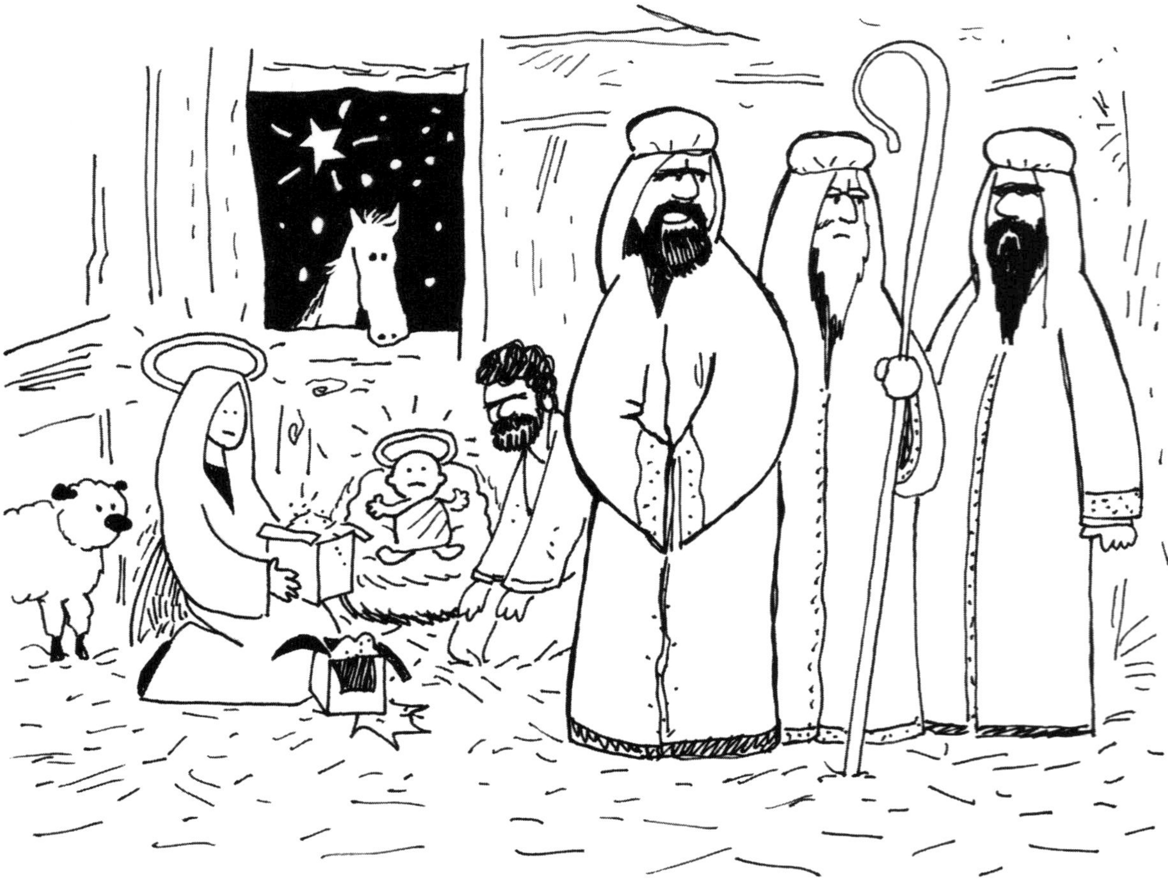

“Frankincense and myrrh?. . . I thought we all agreed on the Diaper Genie.”

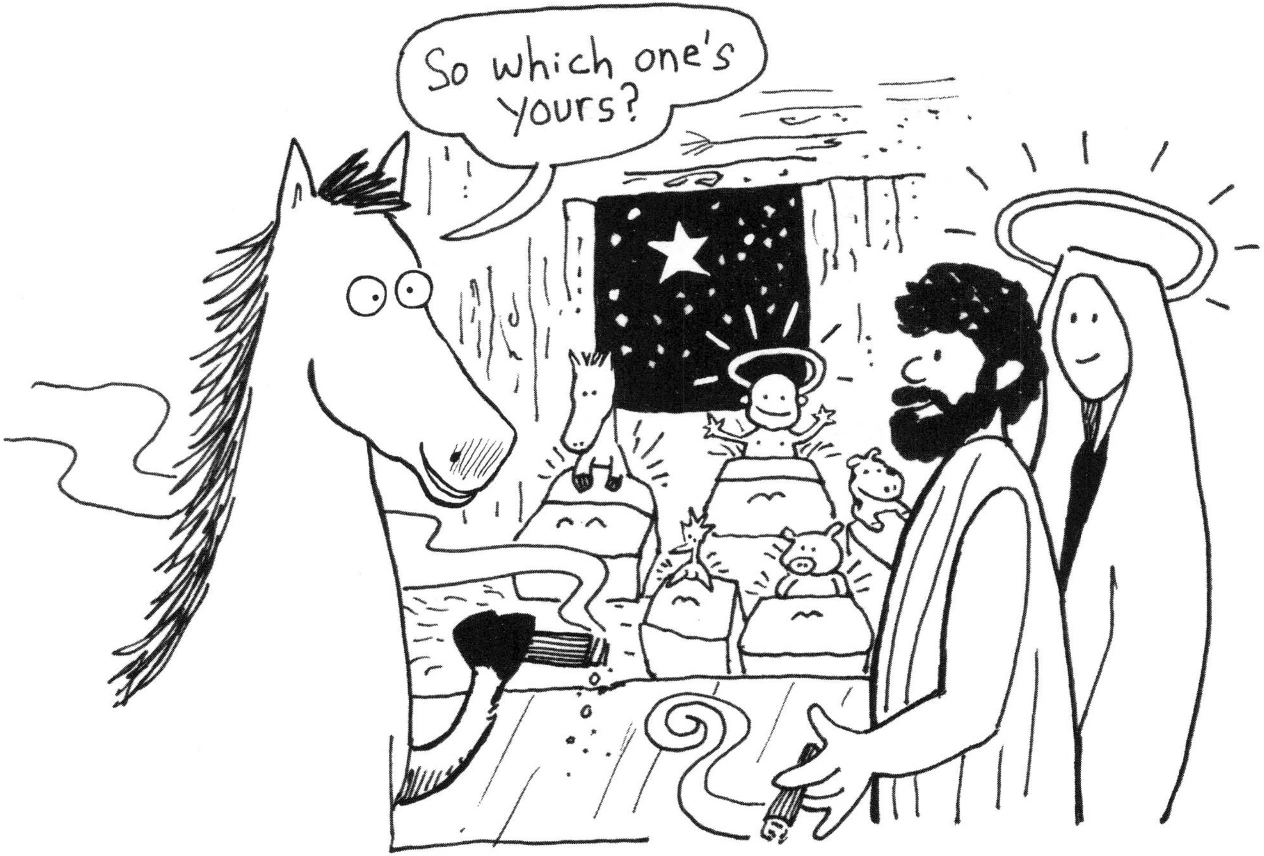
So which one's yours?

The Manger Maternity Ward

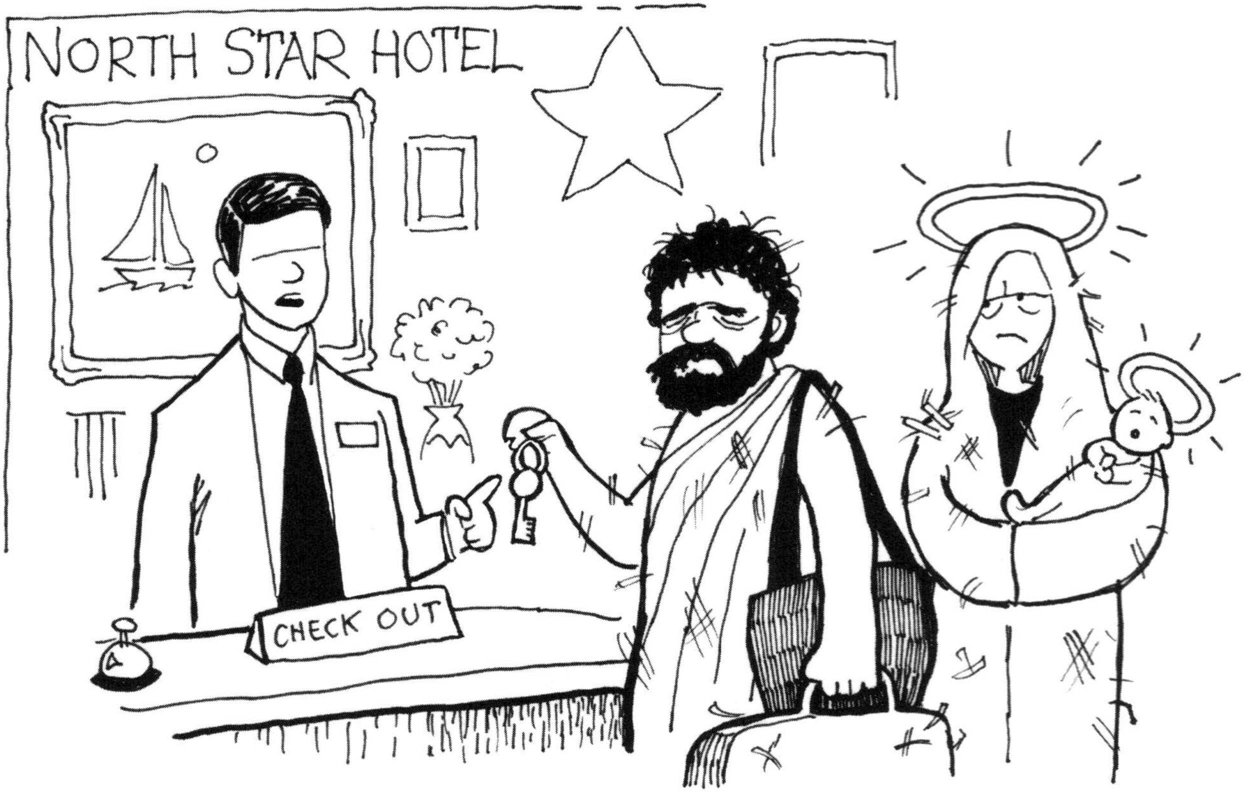
NORTH STAR HOTEL
CHECK OUT

"You slept in the *manger*? I'm afraid you misunderstood, sir.
Those were the keys to the manager's suite."

The First Supper

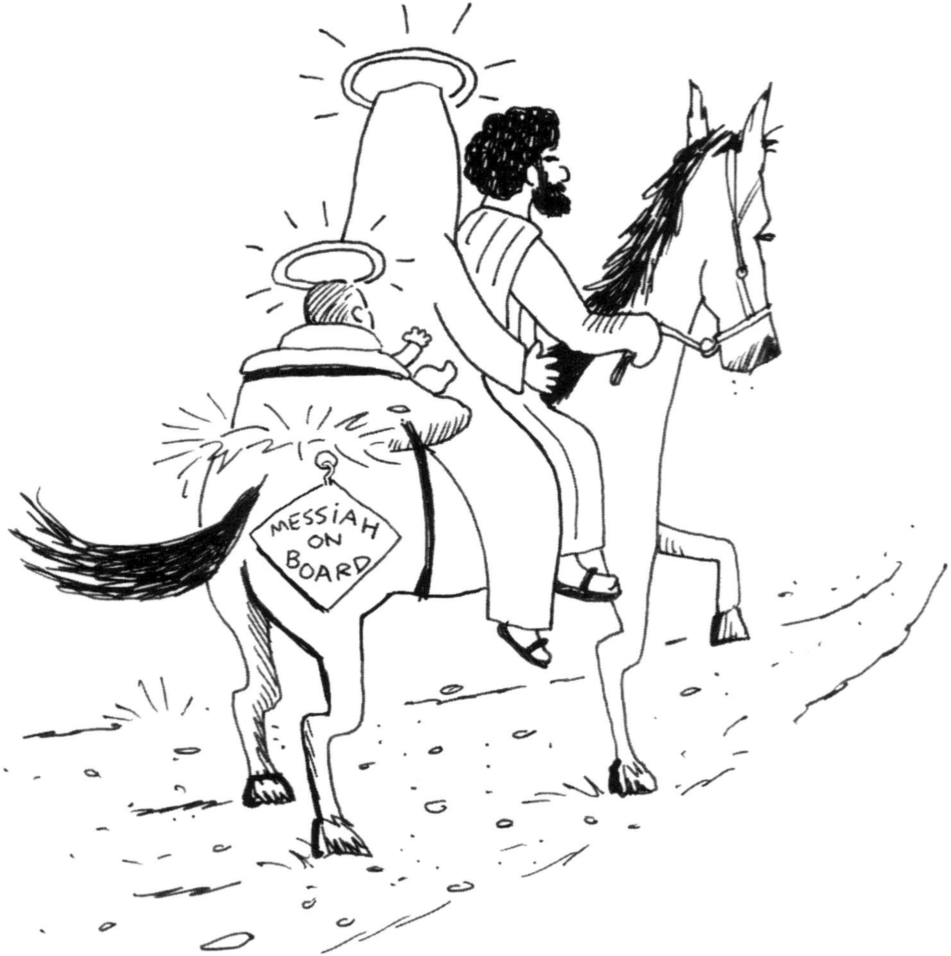
MESSIAH
ON
BOARD

"The least you could do is change a diaper once in a while!"

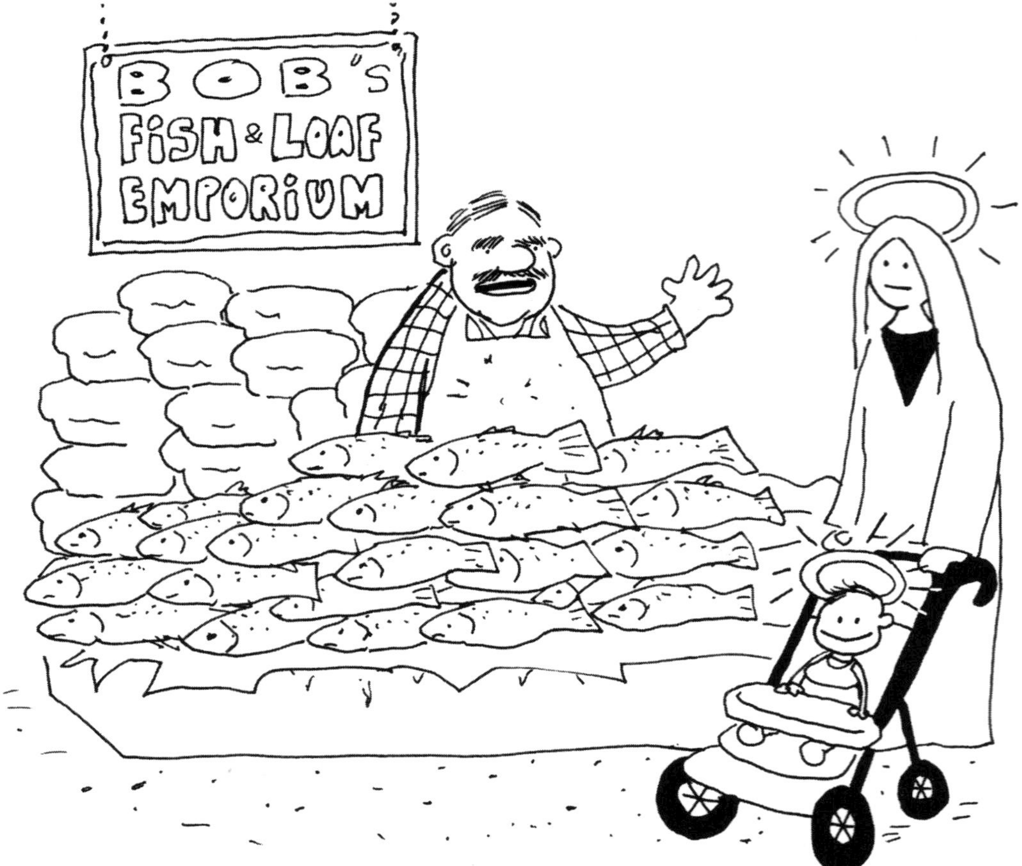
BOB'S
FISH & LOAF
EMPORIUM

"Mary! How come I never see you anymore?
You used to be my best customer!"

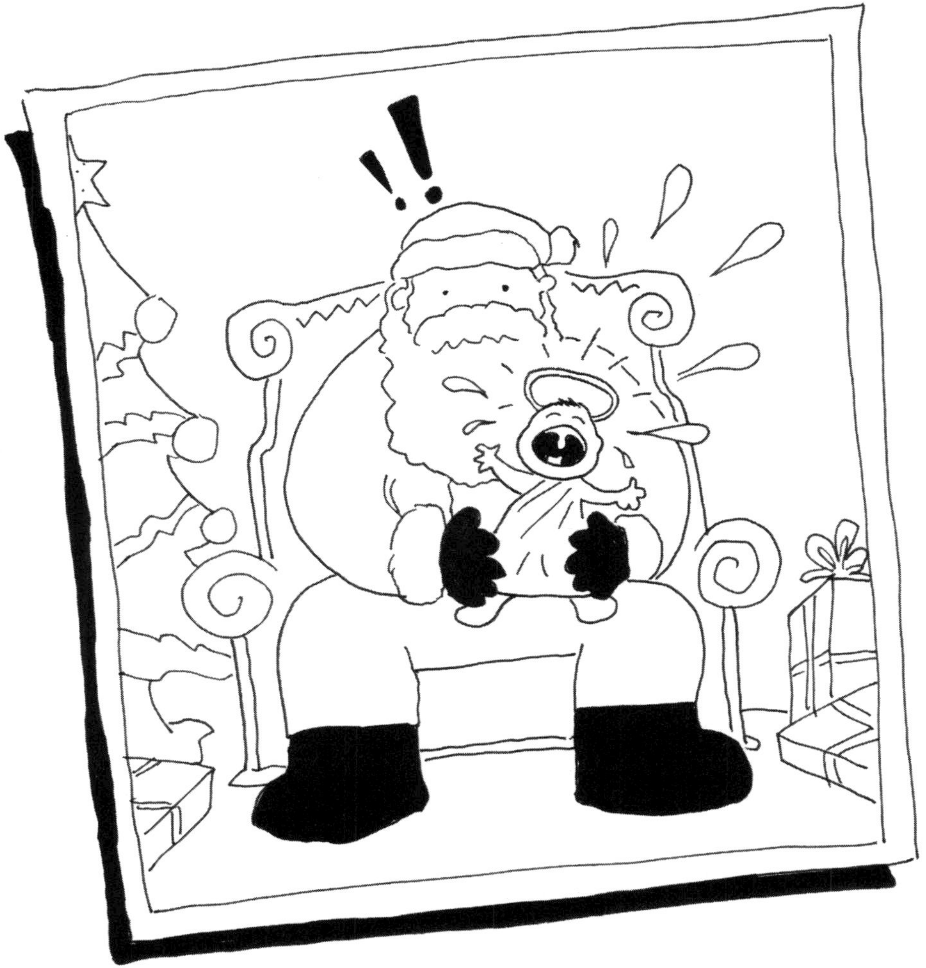

First Steps

The Sippy Cup of Christ

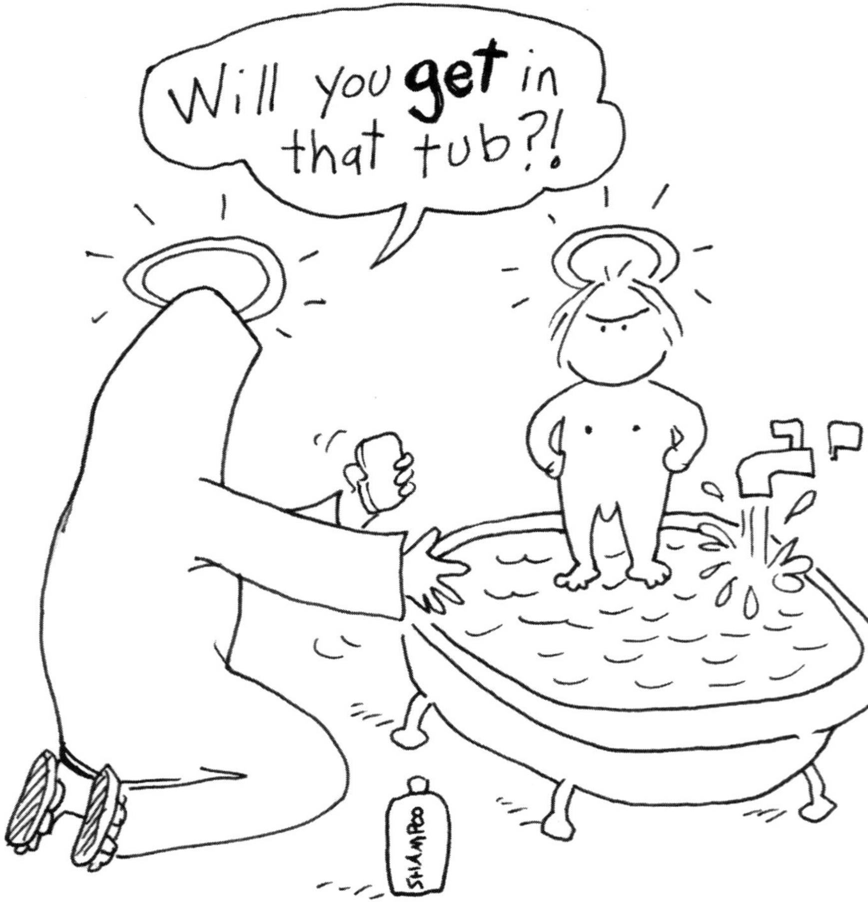
Will you get in that tub?!
SHAMPOO

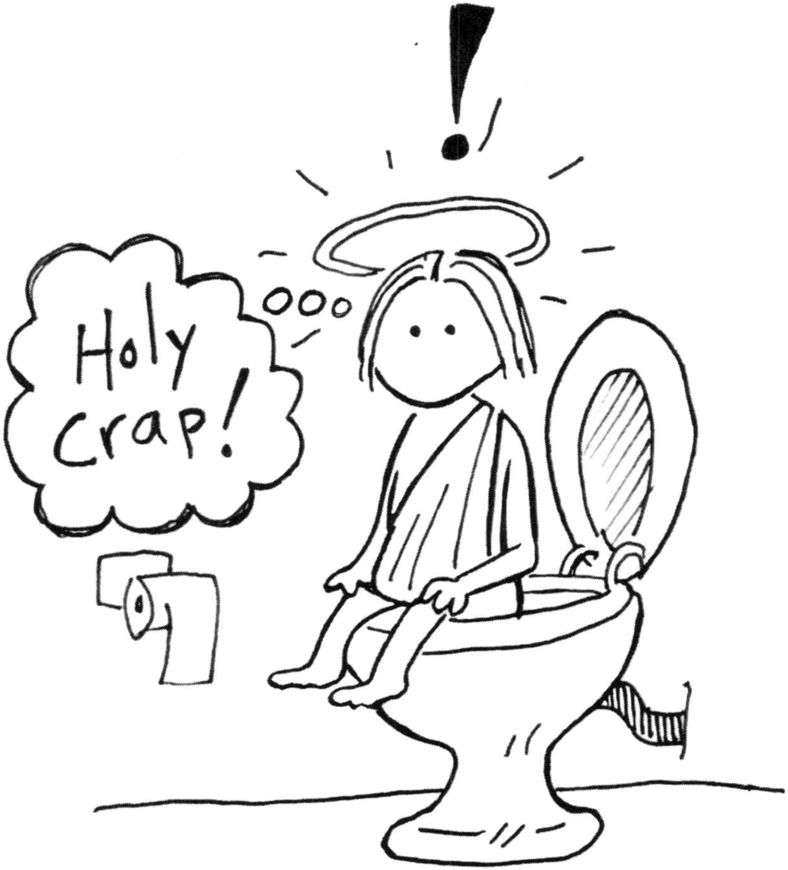
Holy Crap!

"Well, of course no one came to his birthday party—it's Christmas!"

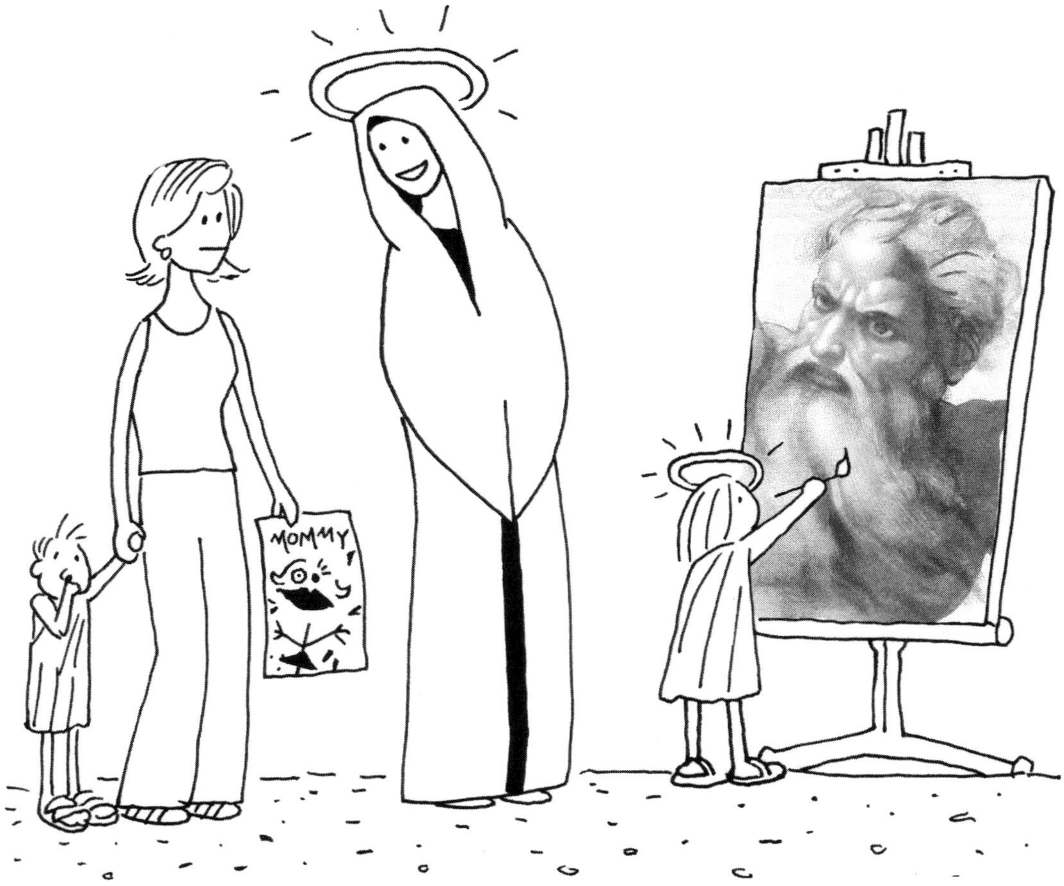
MOMMY

"He gets it from his Father's side."

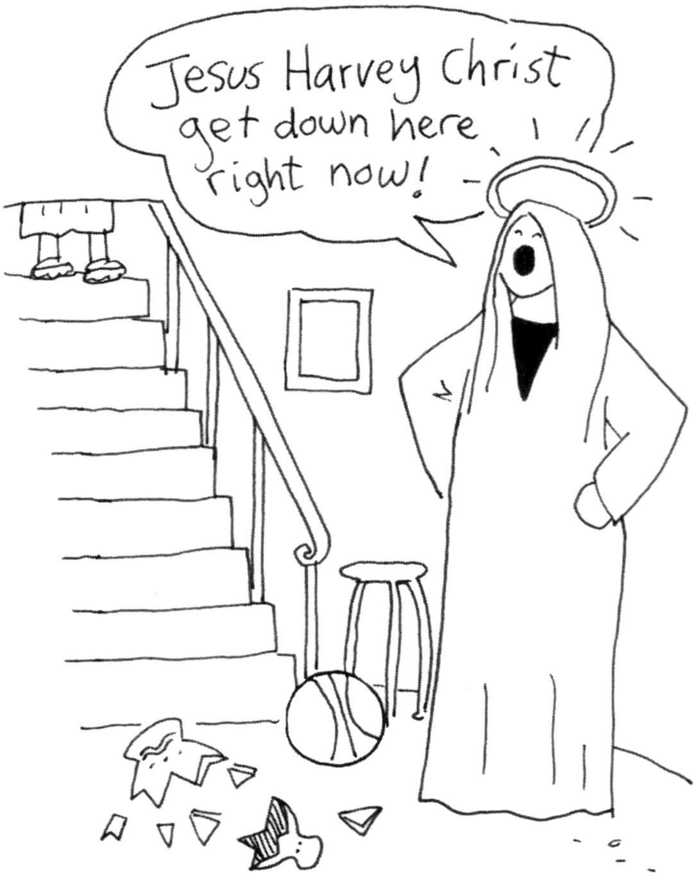
Jesus Harvey Christ get down here right now!

The "H" revealed

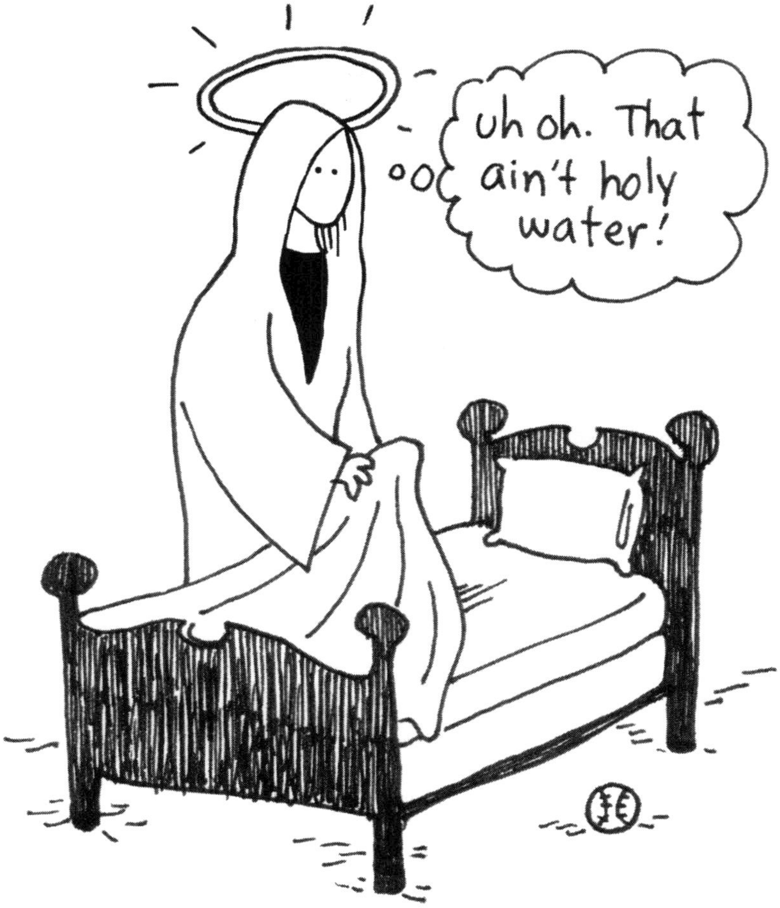
uh oh. That ain't holy water!

VII-XII A.D.

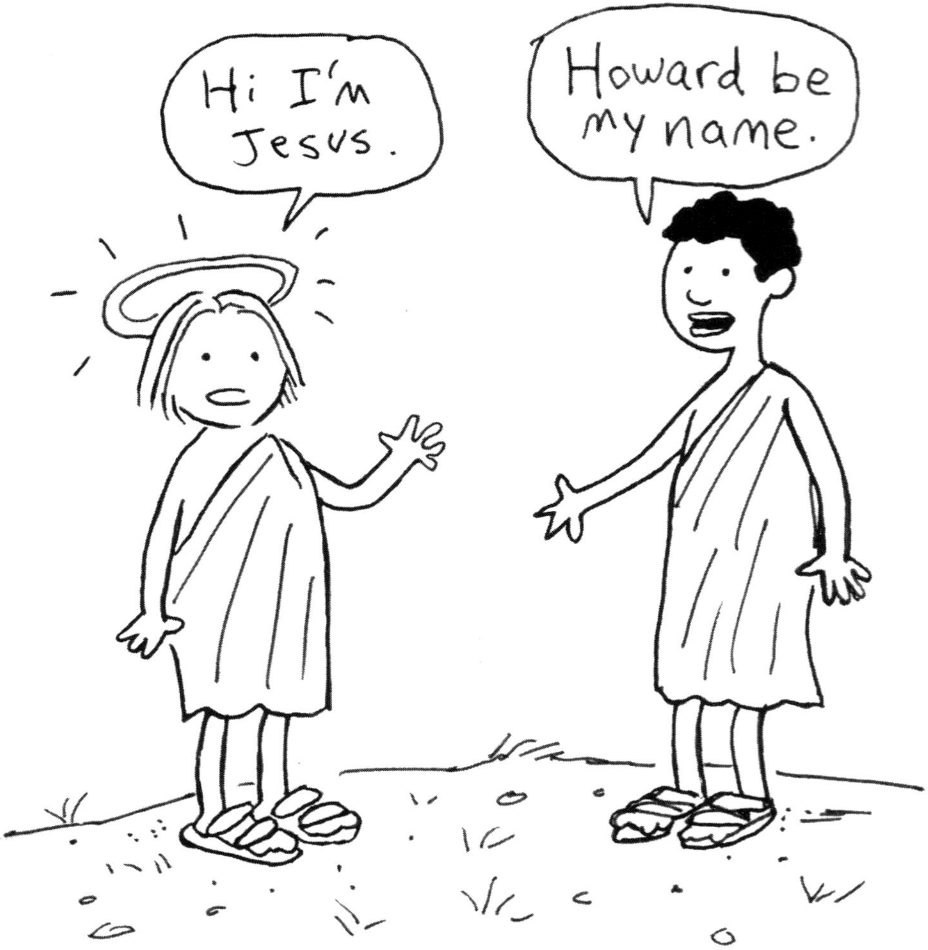
Hi I'm Jesus.
Howard be my name.

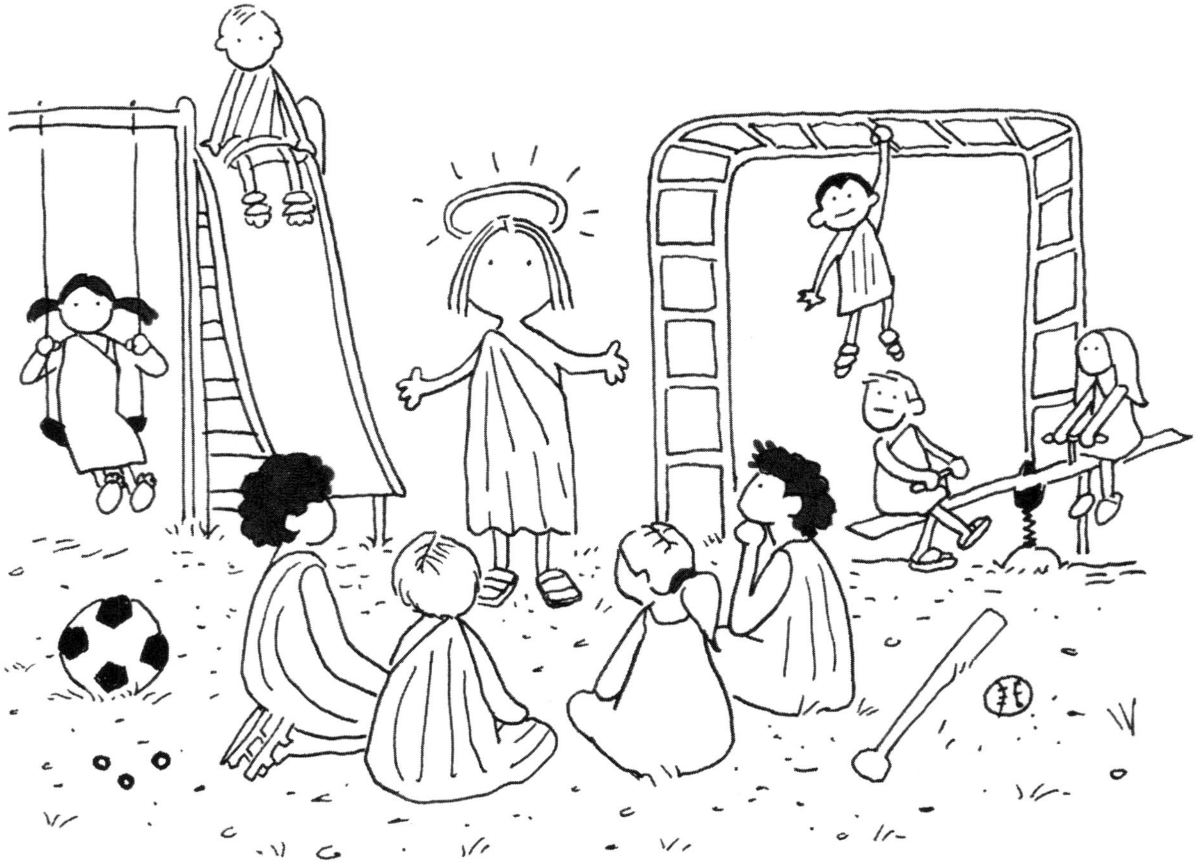

The Sermon at the Jungle Gym

Jesus saves.

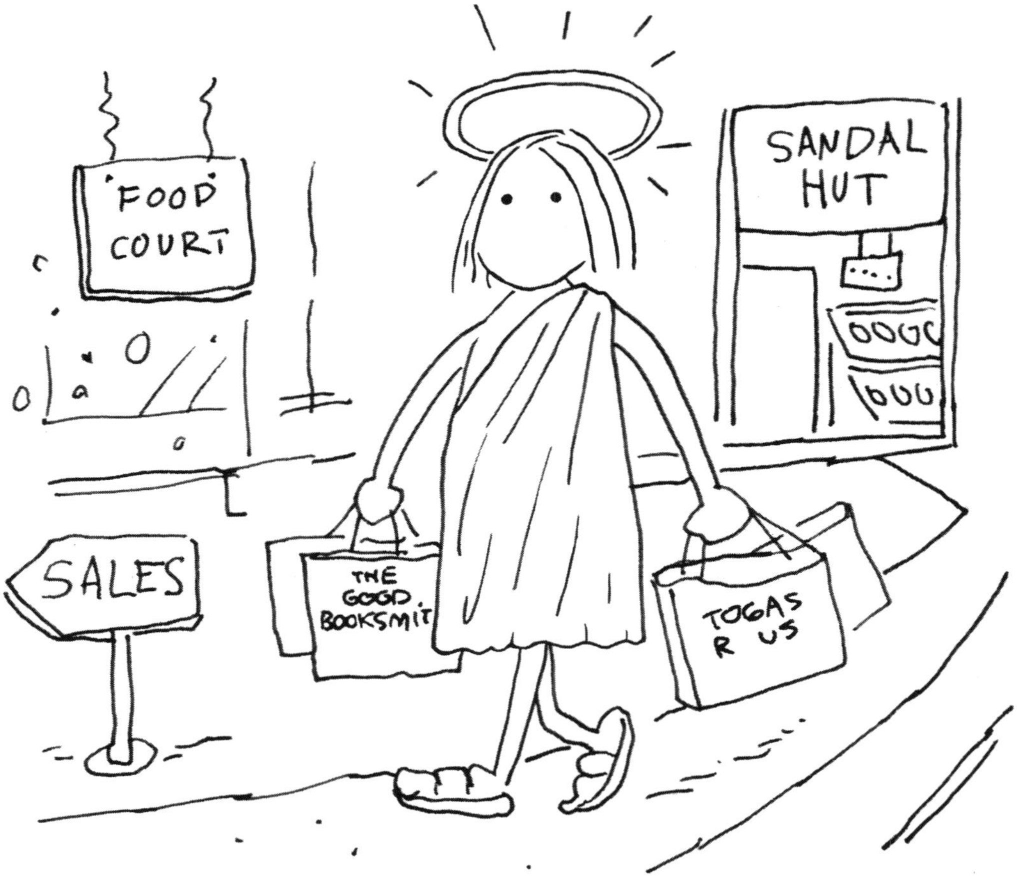
FOOD COURT
SANDAL HUT
SALES
THE GOOD BOOKSMIT
TOGAS R US

Jesus spends.

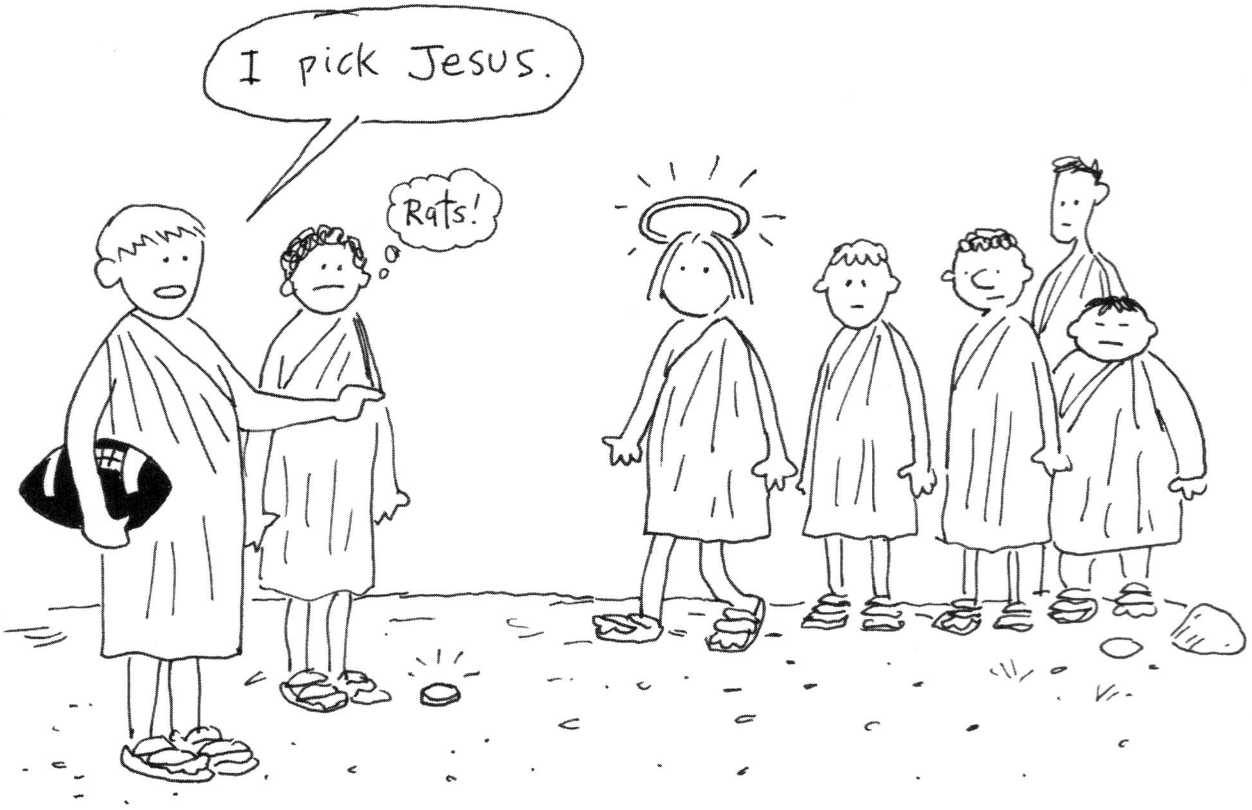
I pick Jesus.
Rats!

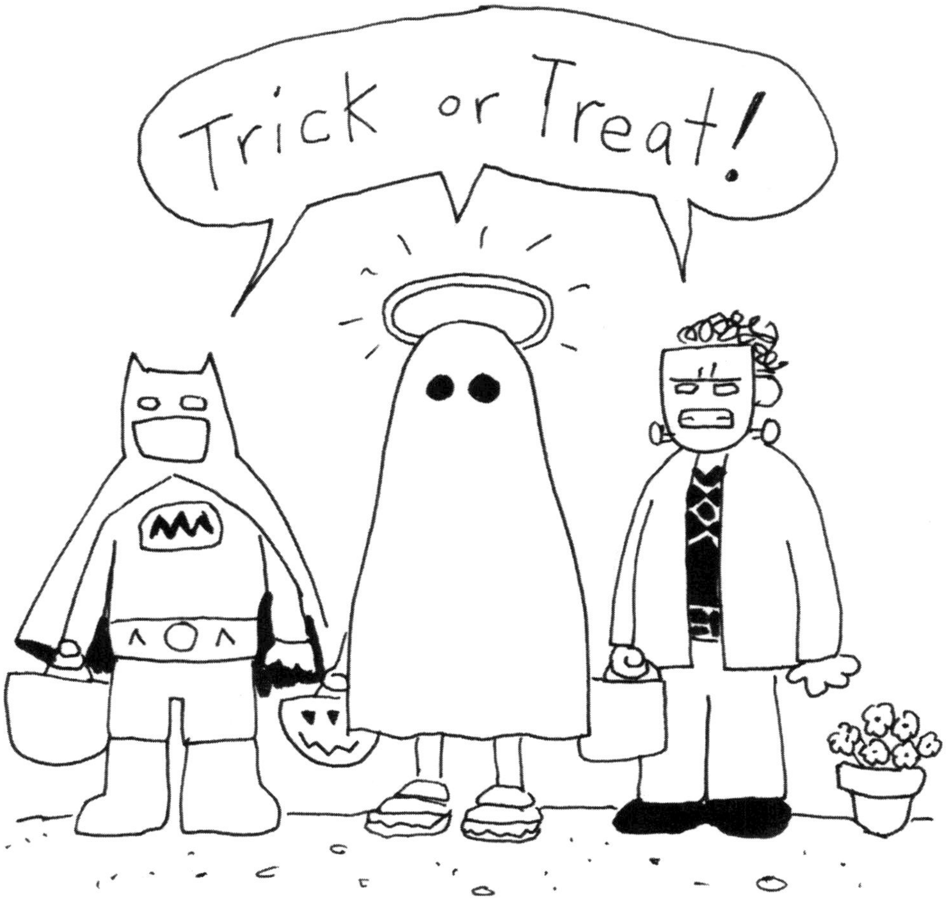
Trick or Treat!

"Now, Jesus . . . God-given talent isn't enough.
You need to practice, practice, practice!"

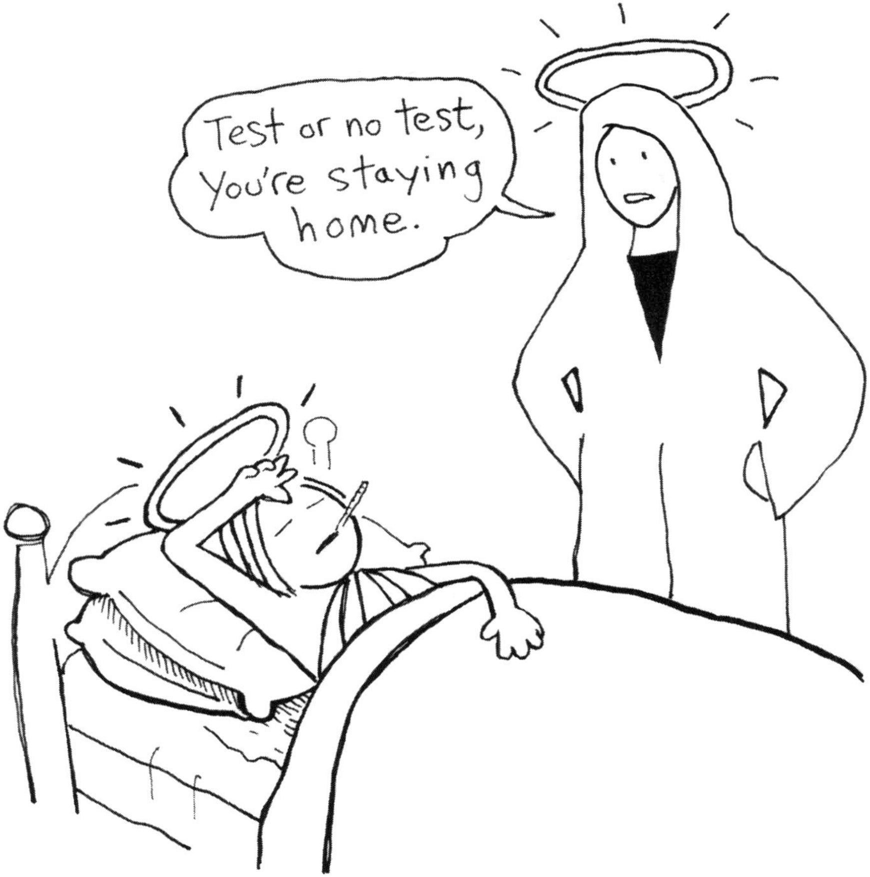
Test or no test, you're staying home.

No one could fake sick like Jesus.

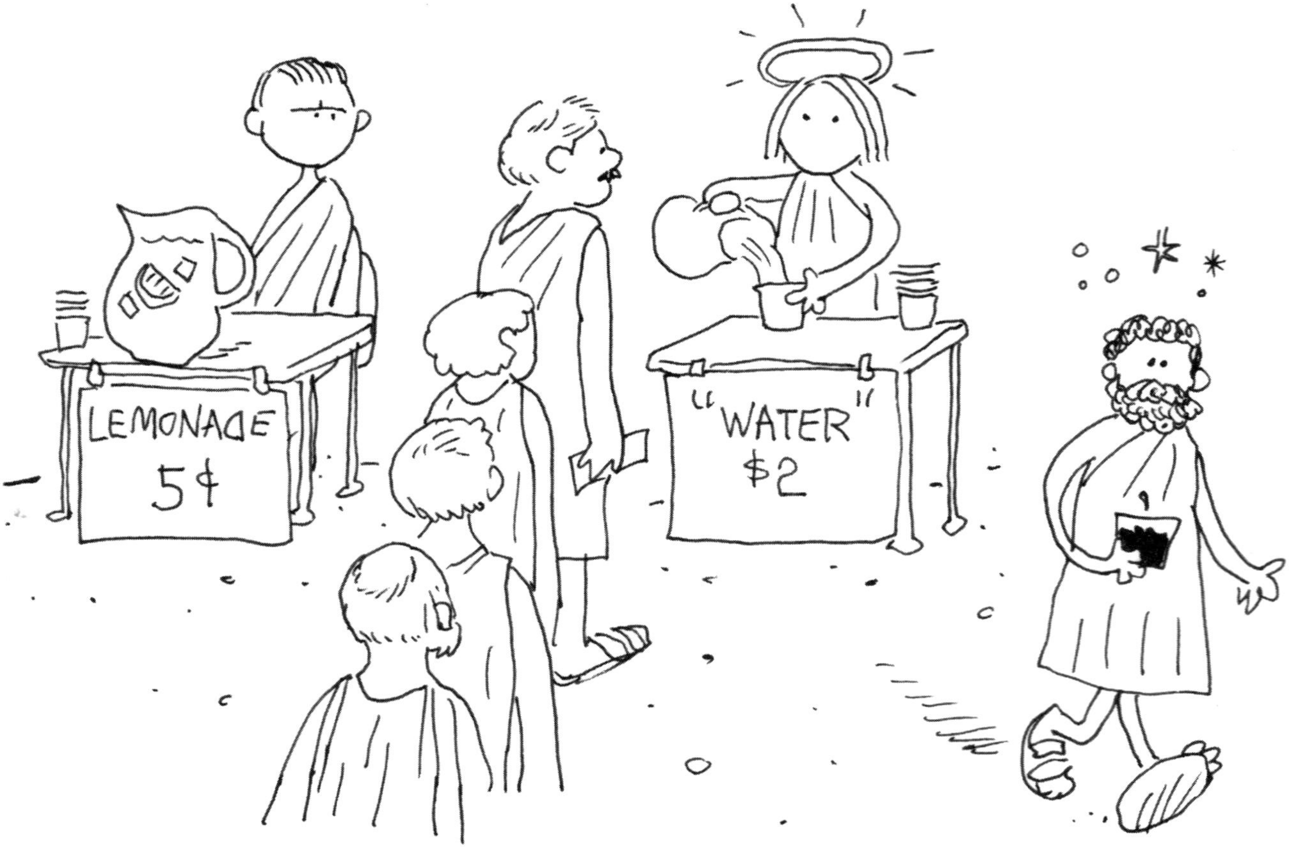
LEMONADE
5¢
"WATER"
$2

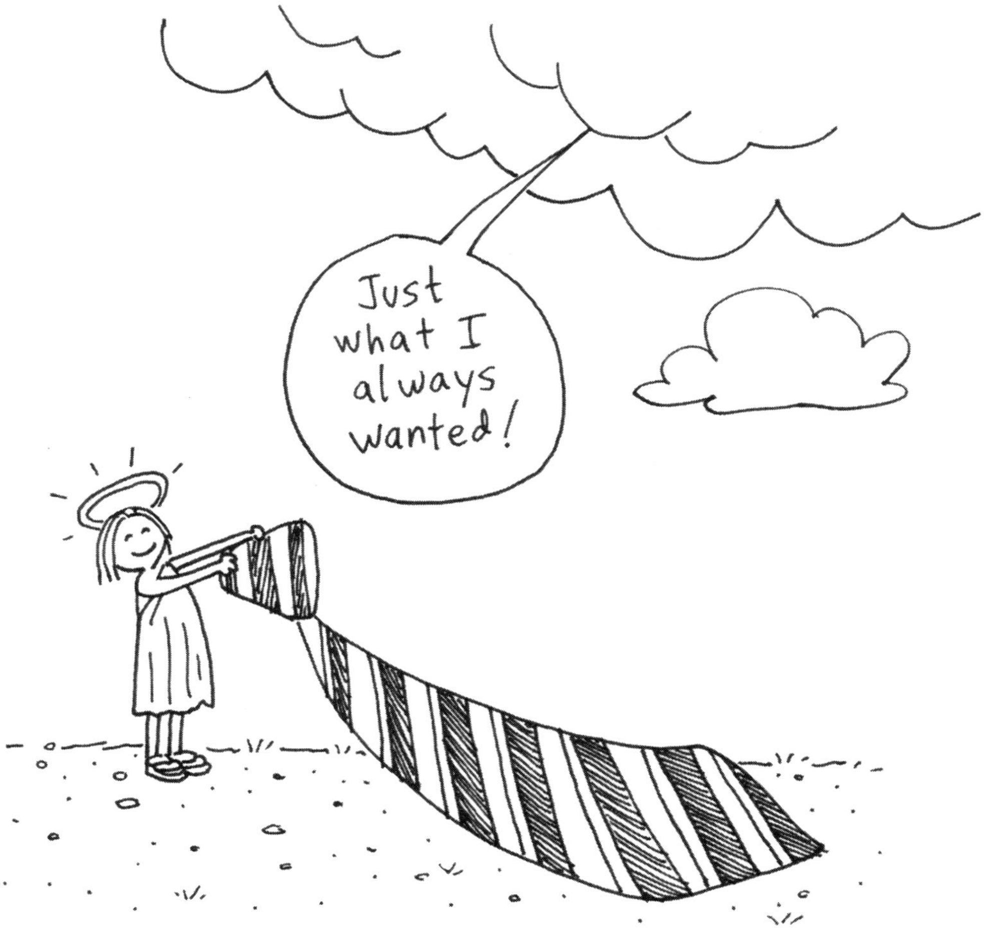
Just what I always wanted!

Father's Day

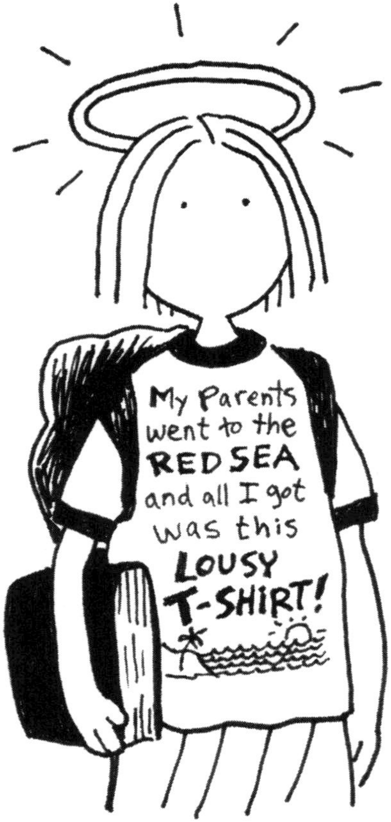
My Parents went to the RED SEA and all I got was this LOUSY T-SHIRT!

Before he was tempted by the devil in the desert,
Jesus was tempted by the devil's food cake dessert.

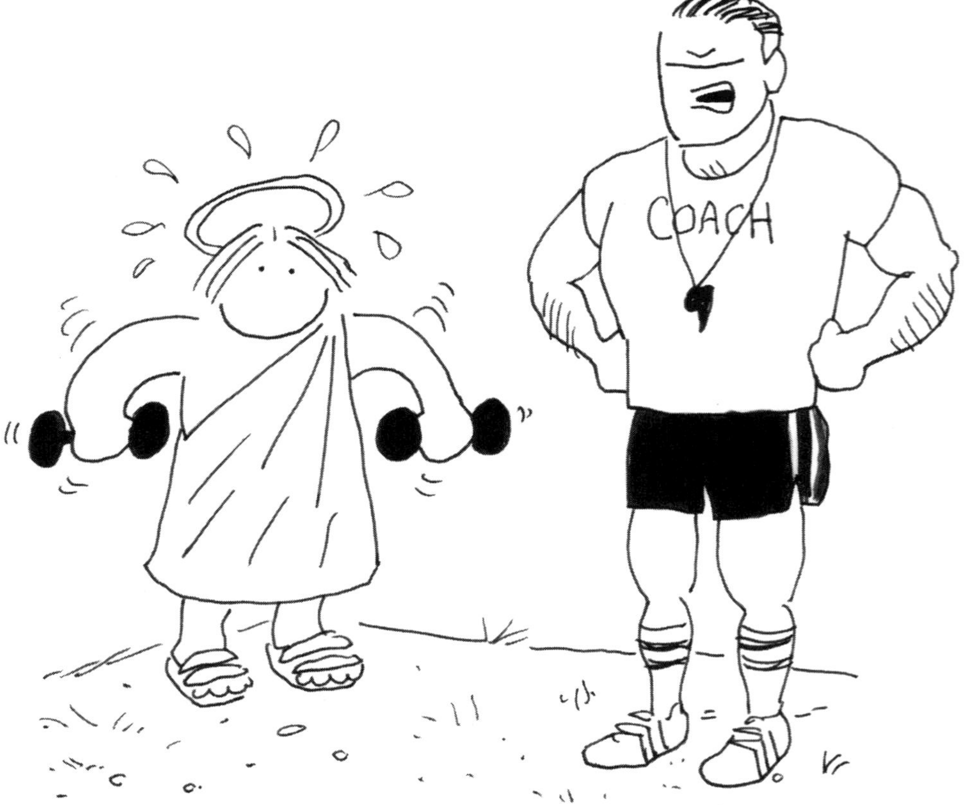
COACH

"Oh sure, you can turn water into wine. Let's see you turn fat into muscle, chubby!"

Holy Roller

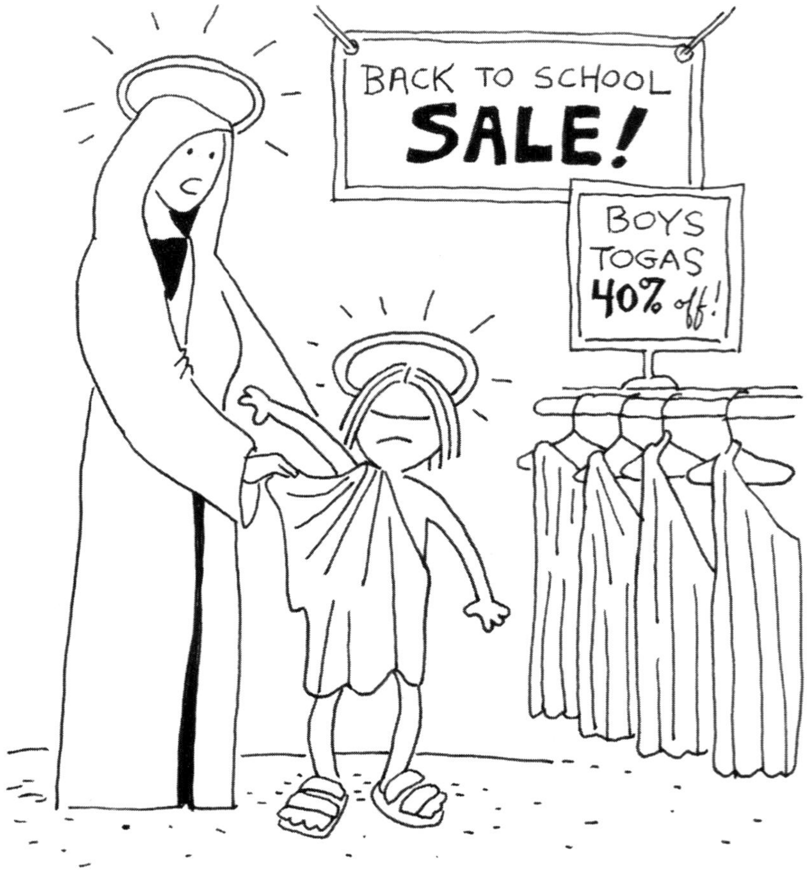
BACK TO SCHOOL
SALE!
BOYS
TOGAS
40% off!

"I don't care what all the other kids are wearing.
Now put this on!"

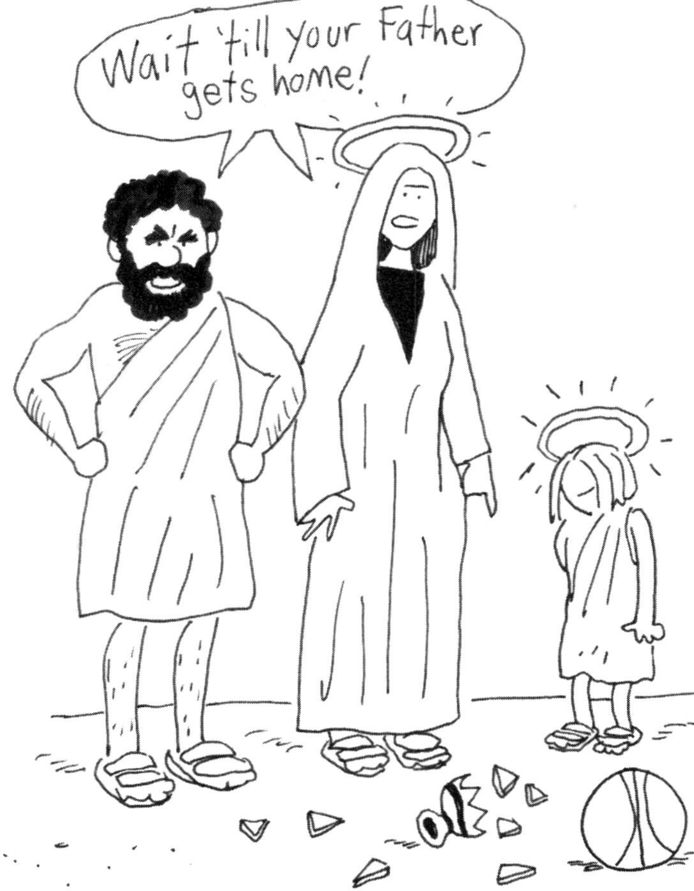
Wait 'till your Father gets home!

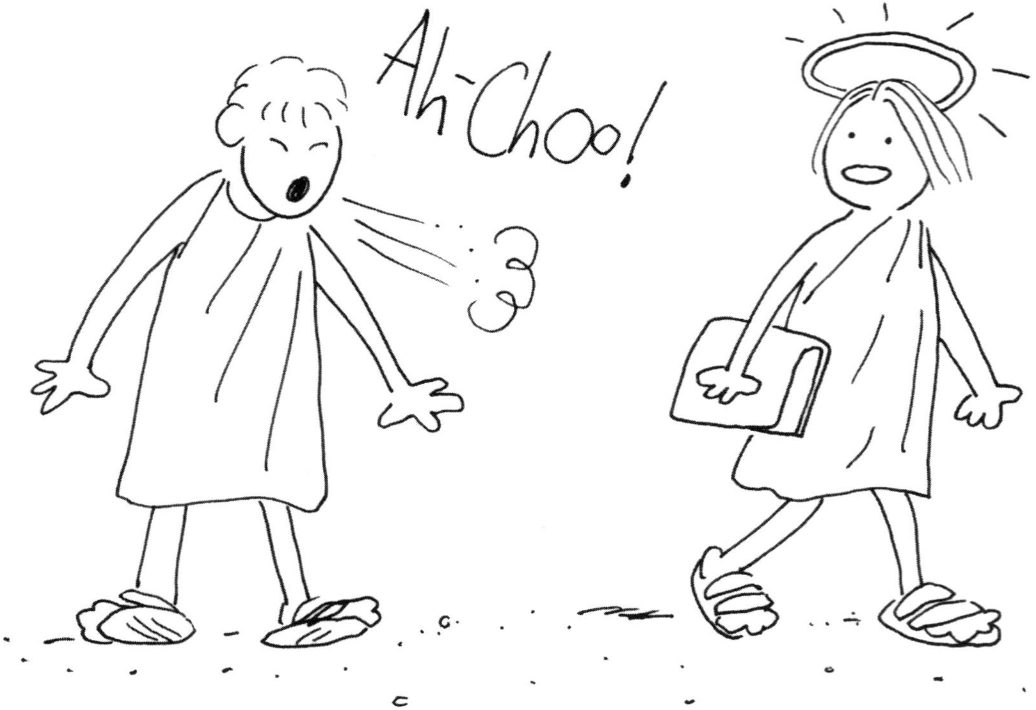
Ah-Choo!

"Dad bless you."

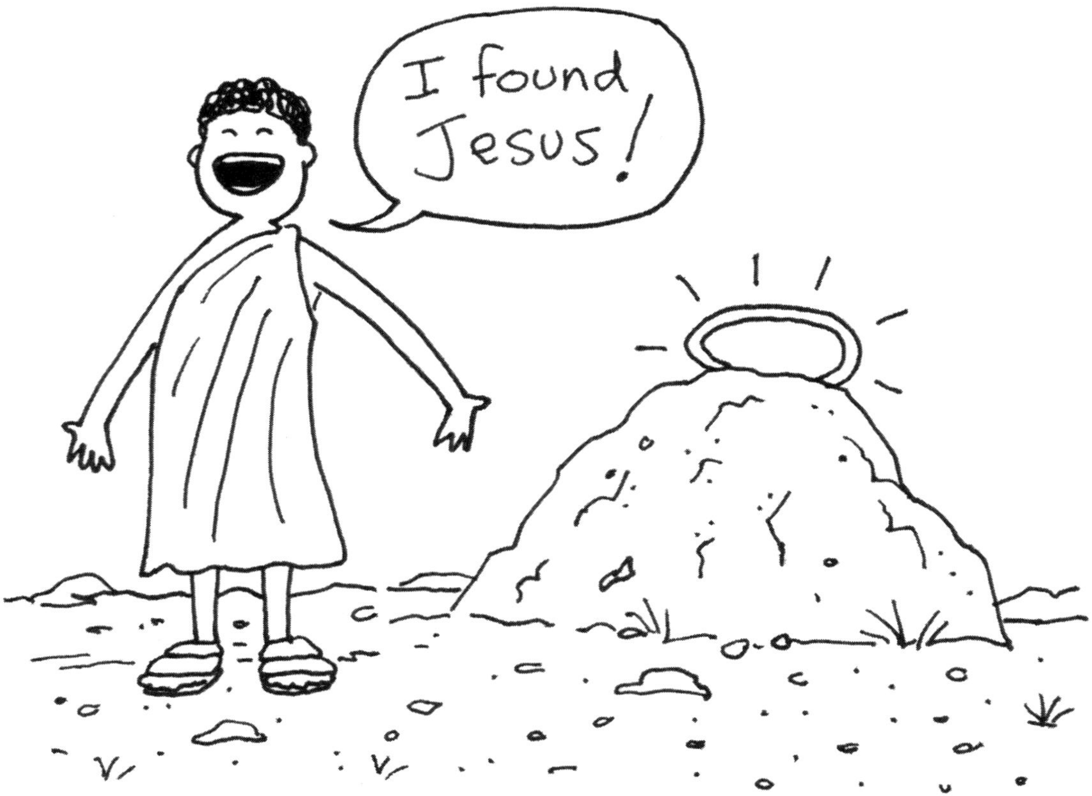
I found Jesus!

Hide and Seek

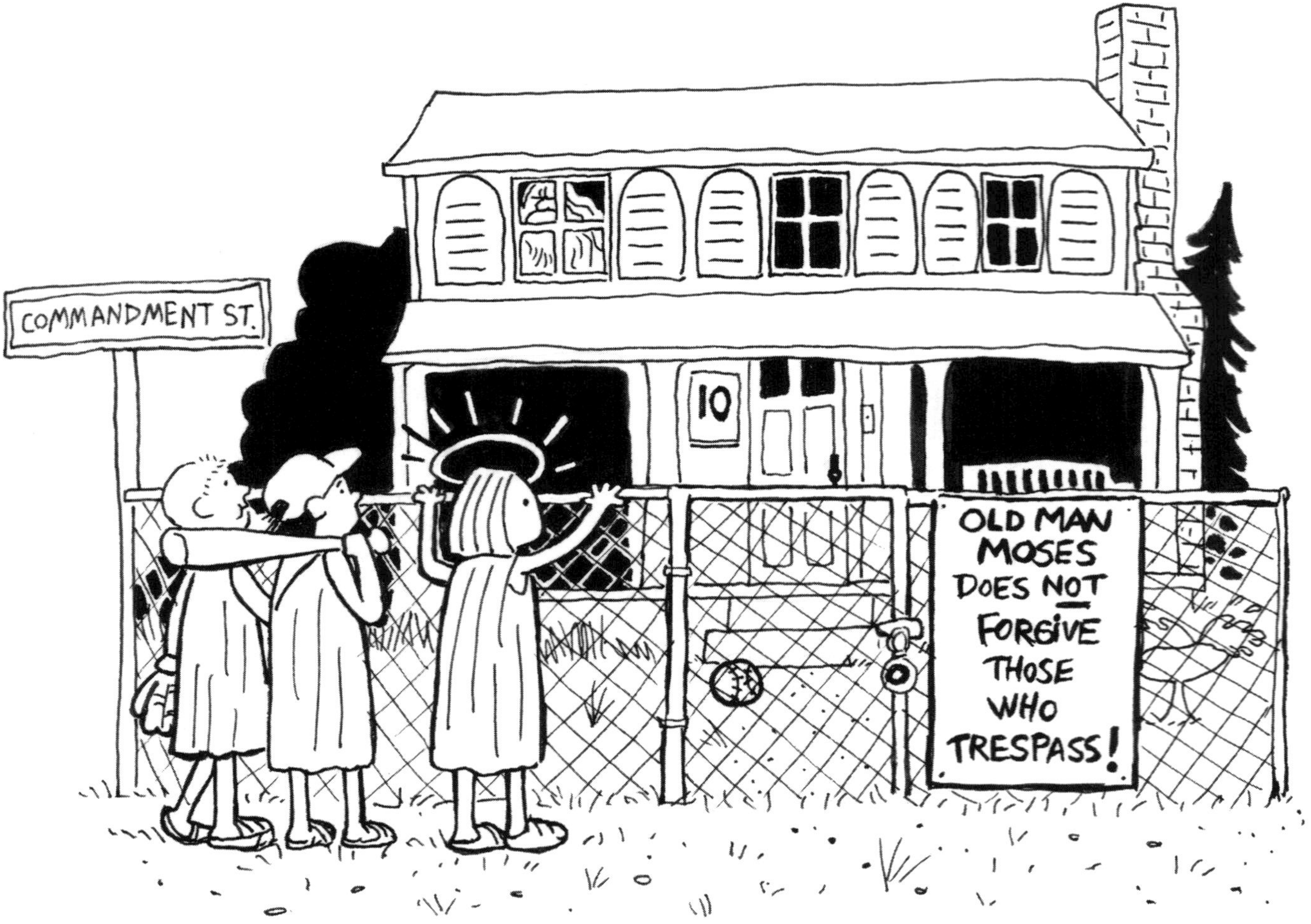
COMMANDMENT ST.
10
OLD MAN MOSES DOES NOT FORGIVE THOSE WHO TRESPASS!

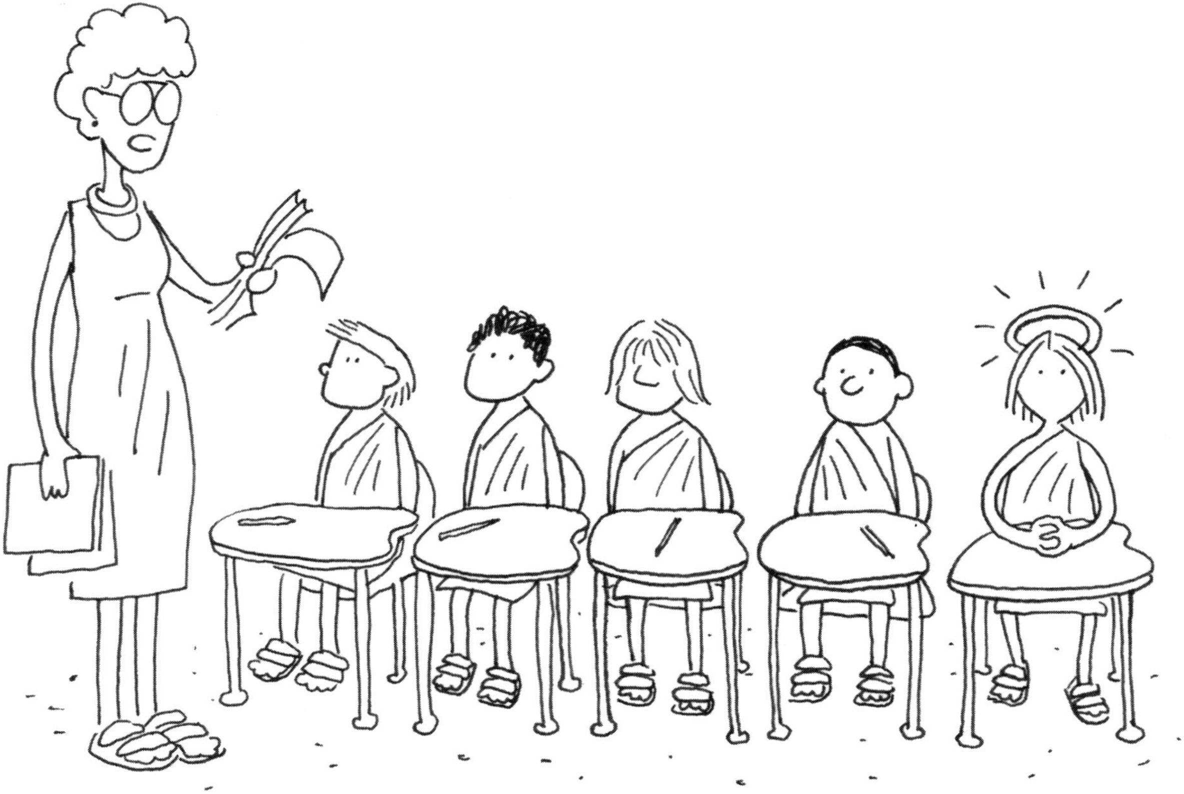

“Matthew, Mark, Luke, and John, see me after class. Your book reports are surprisingly similar.”

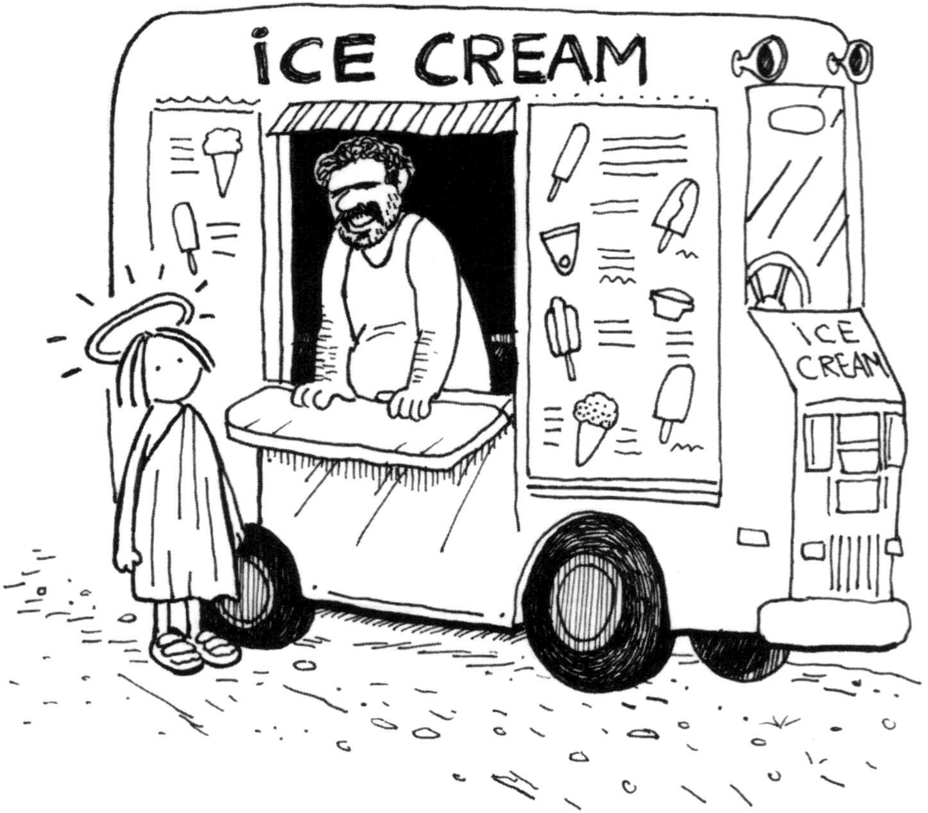
ICE CREAM
ICE CREAM

“Palm sundae? Never heard of it. How about an Italian ice?”

"Stairway to Heaven" was always the last song at the
Nazareth Middle School dances.

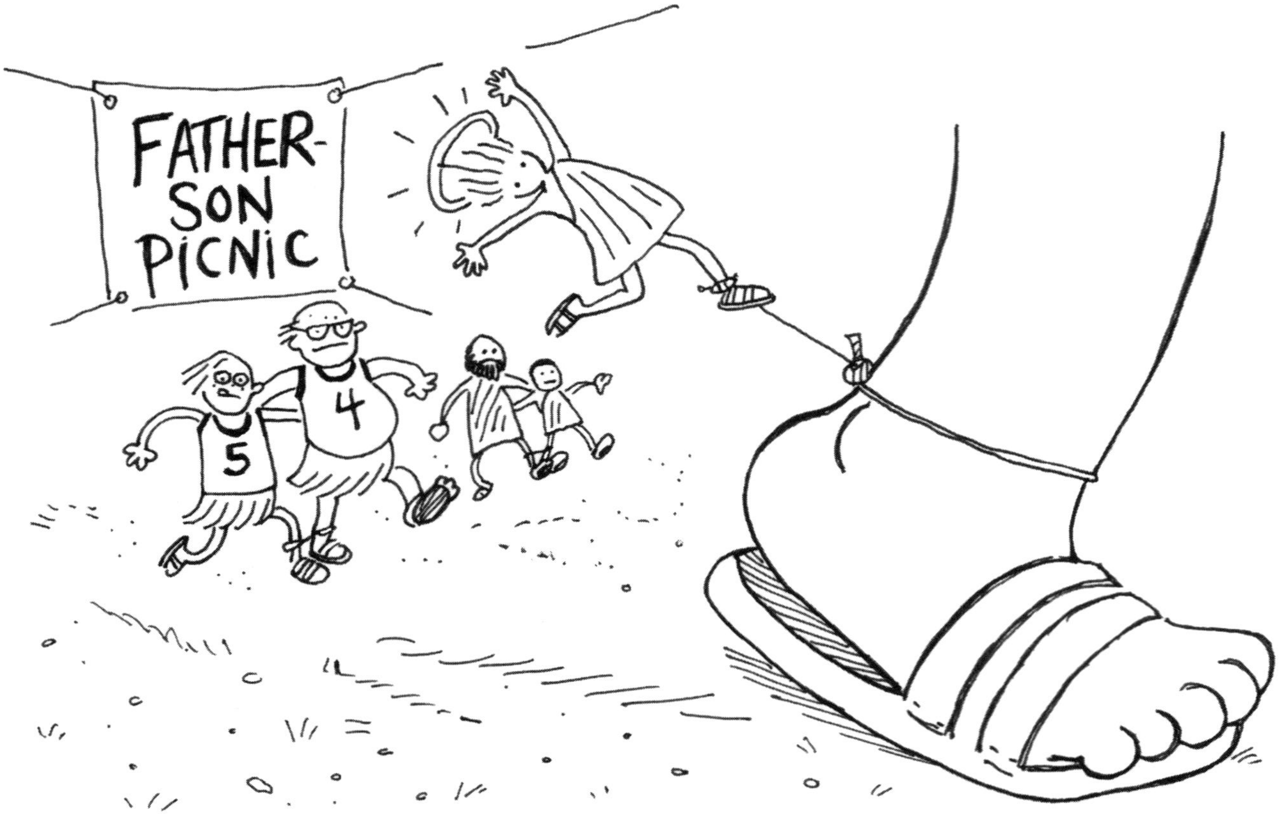
FATHER-
SON
PICNIC
5
4

"Give us this day your daily lunch money!"

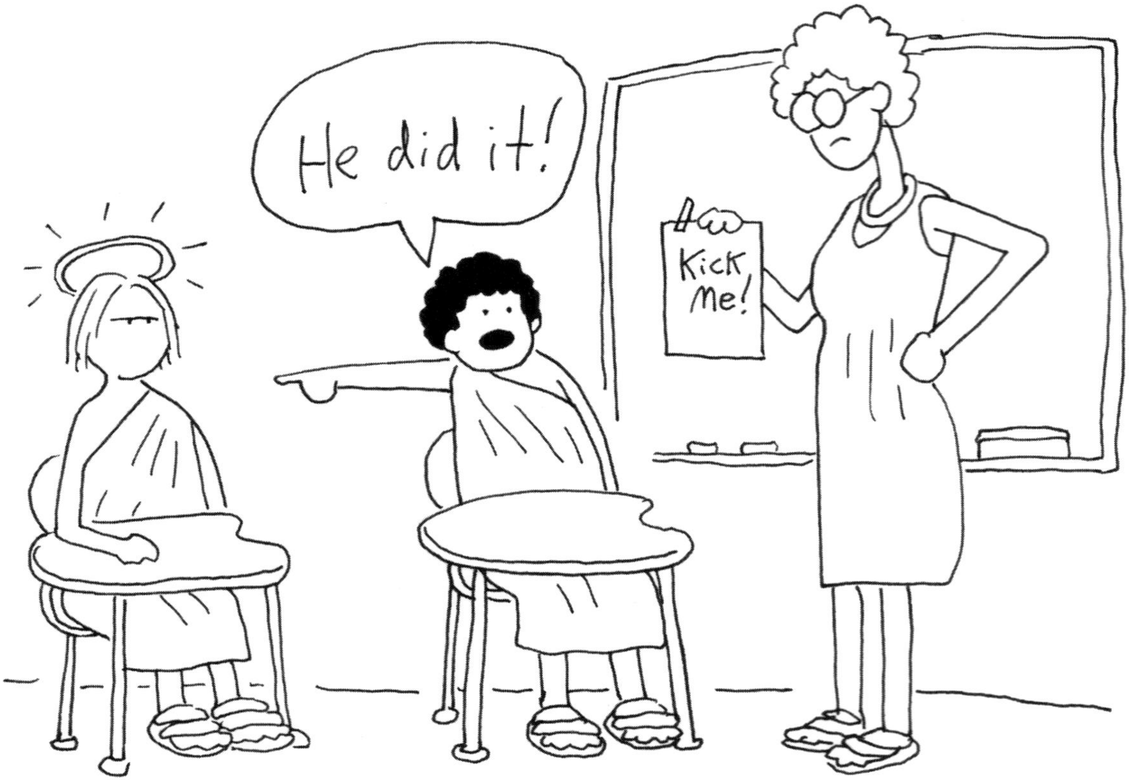
He did it!
Kick me!

Jesus's first encounter with Judas.

Spin the Goblet

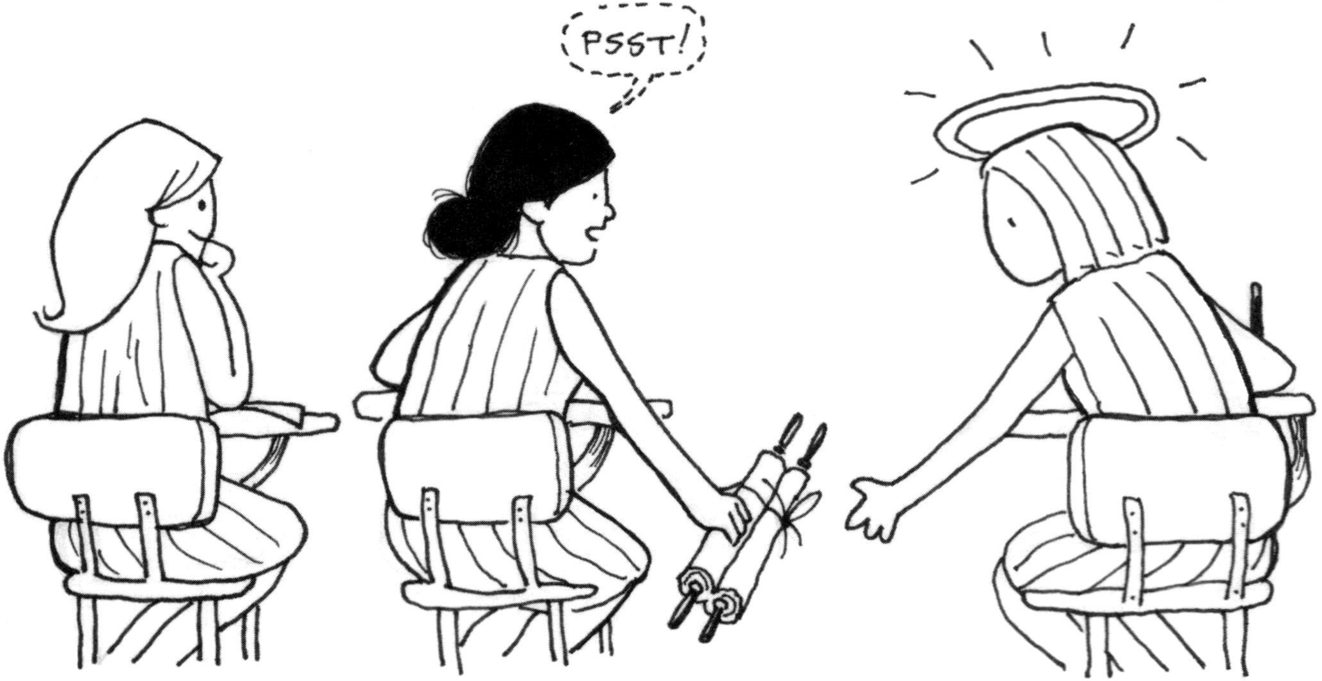
PSST!

Passing Scrolls in Class

The Original Soccer Mom

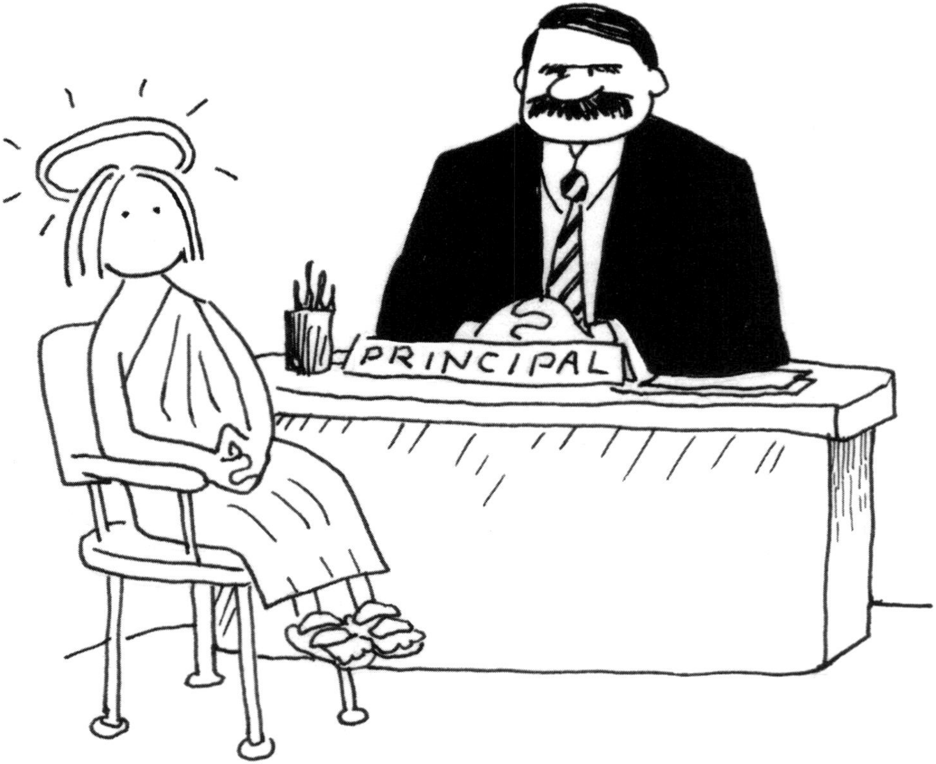
PRINCIPAL

“That was a very impressive sermon about turning the other cheek, Jesus. But I’m still giving you a week’s detention.”

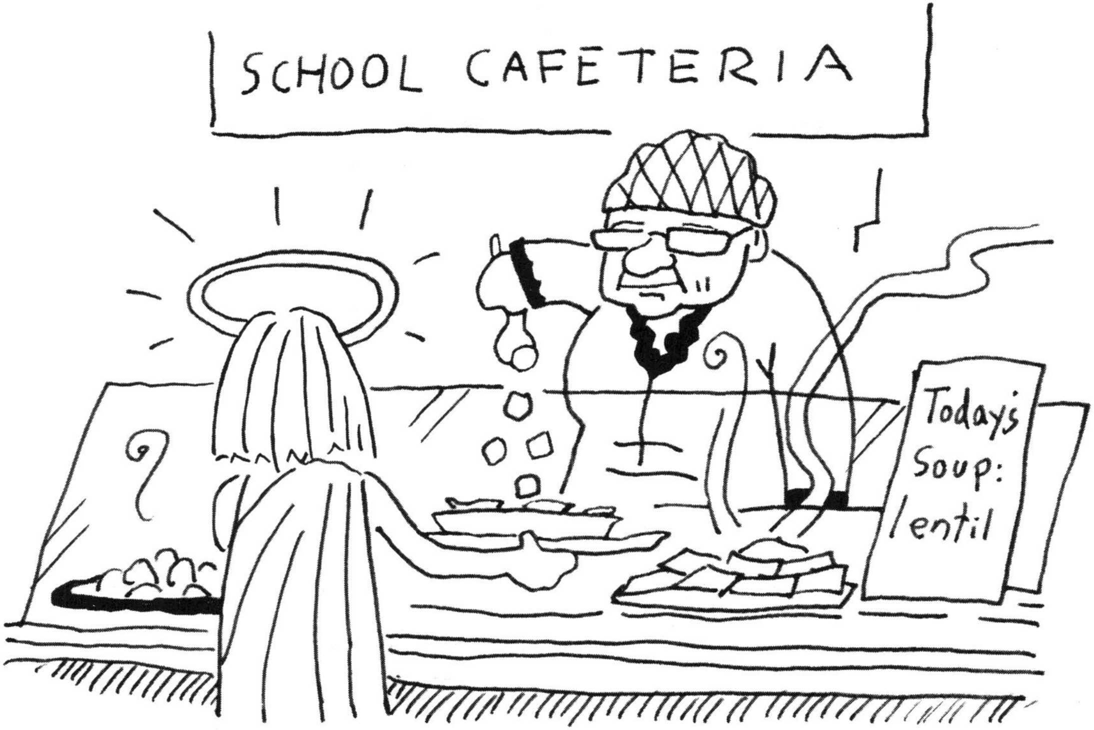
SCHOOL CAFETERIA
Todays Soup: lentil

And when He was hungry, she gave Him meat ravioli with tater tots.

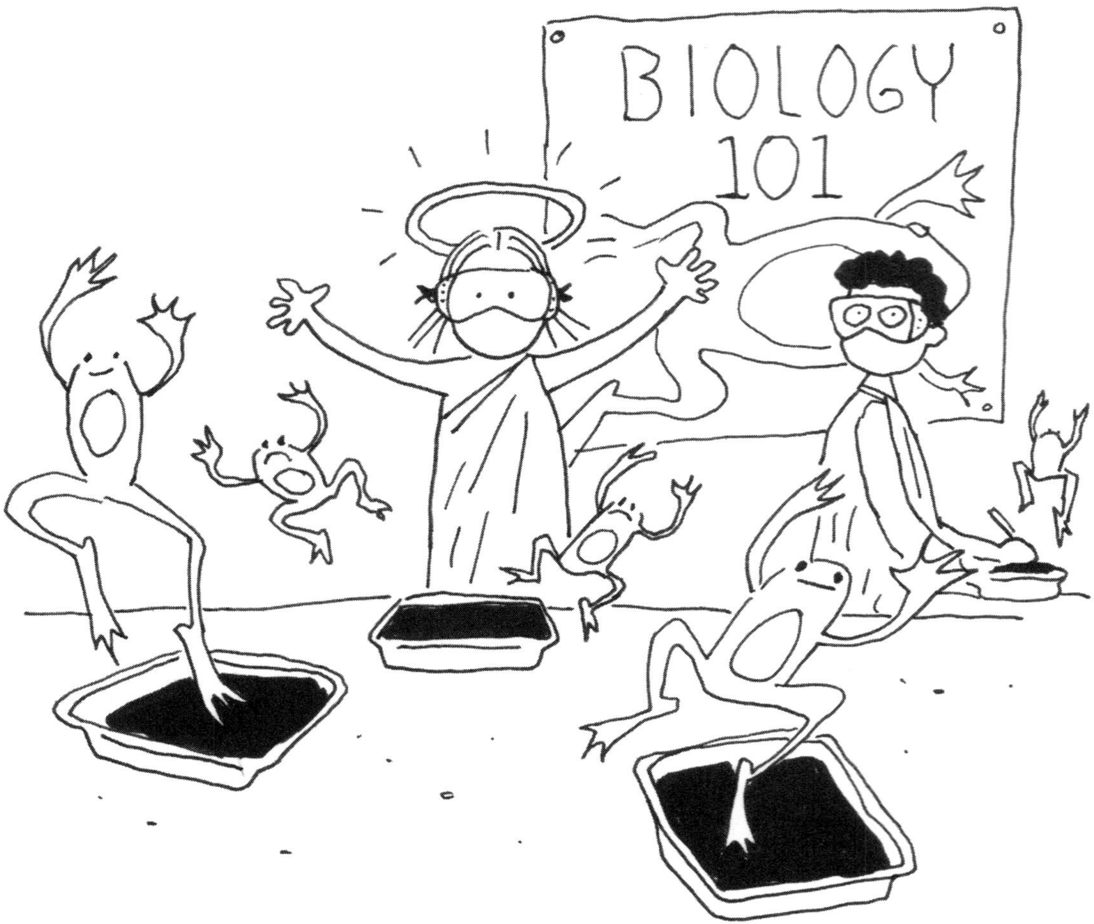
BIOLOGY
101

Lesser-Known Miracle #1: The Raising of the Frogs

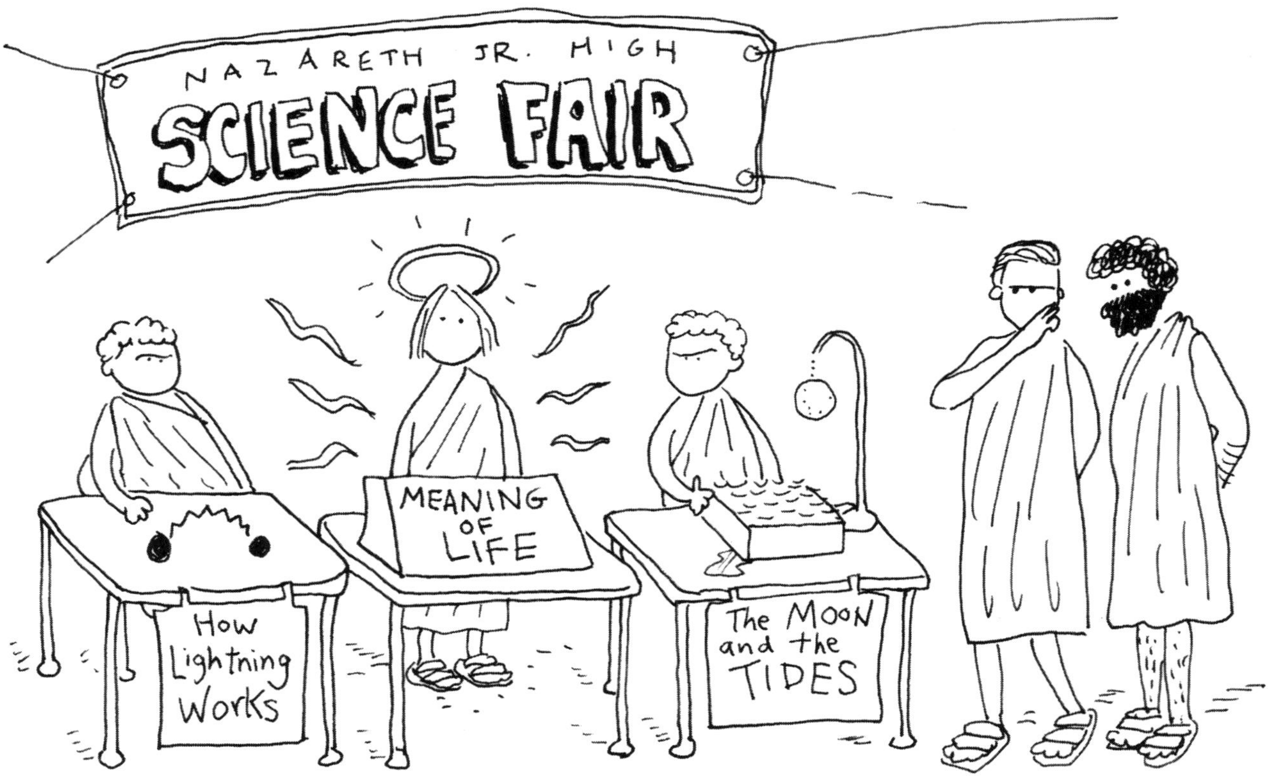
NAZARETH JR. HIGH
SCIENCE FAIR
MEANING OF LIFE
How Lightning Works
The MOON and the TIDES

"I suspect a little help from Dad on this one."

XIII-XVIII A.D.

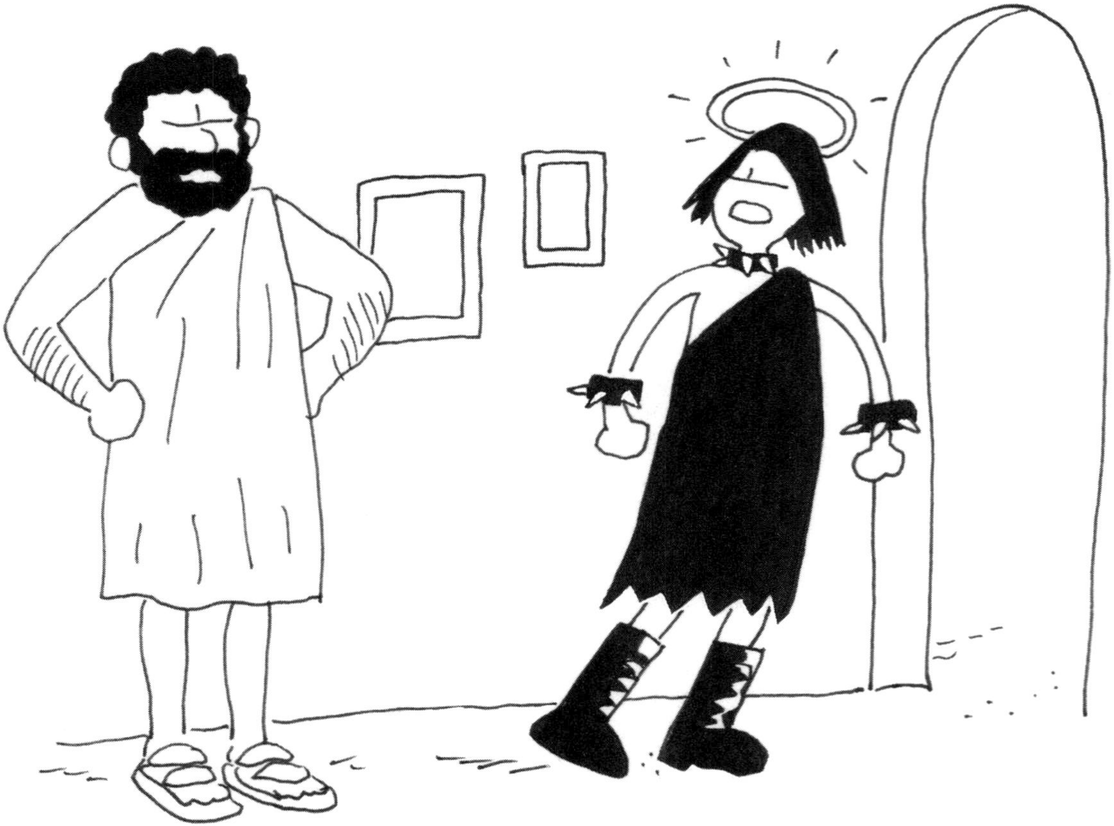

"You can't tell me what to do! You're not my Father!"

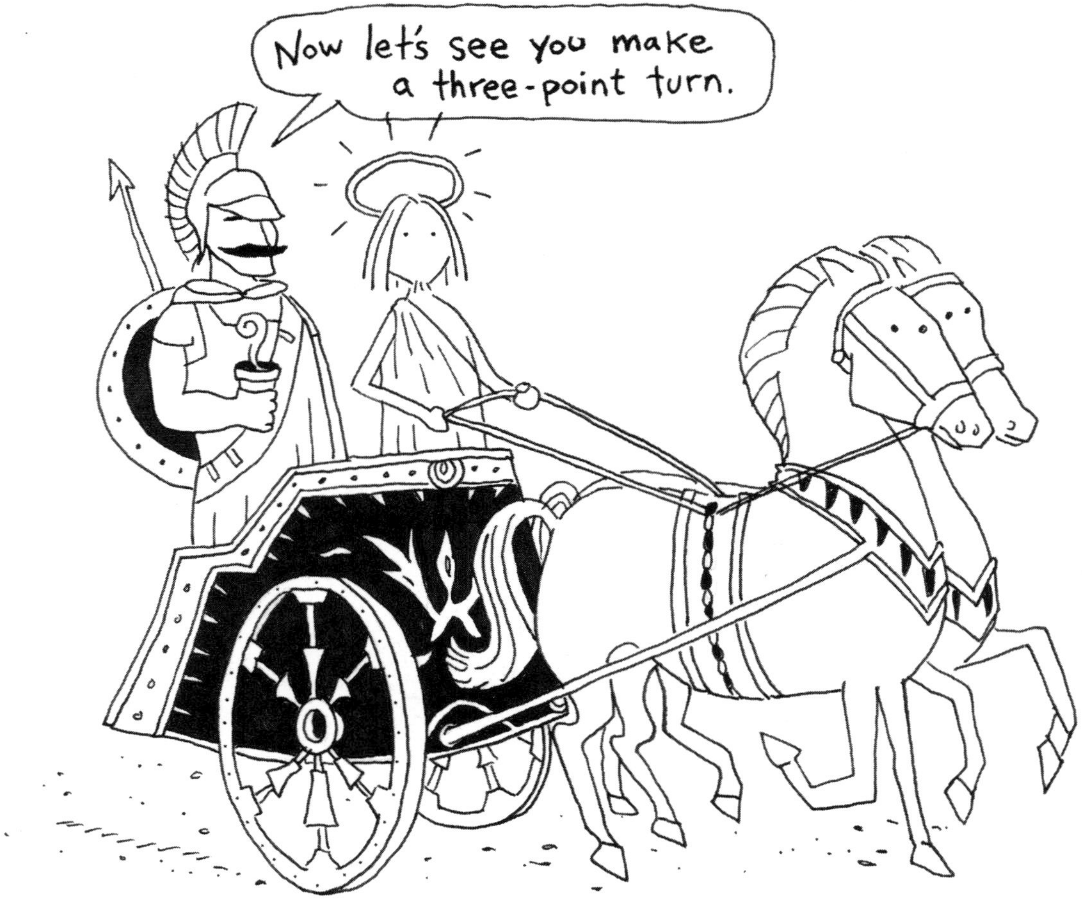
Now let's see you make a three-point turn.

Chariot Driver's Ed

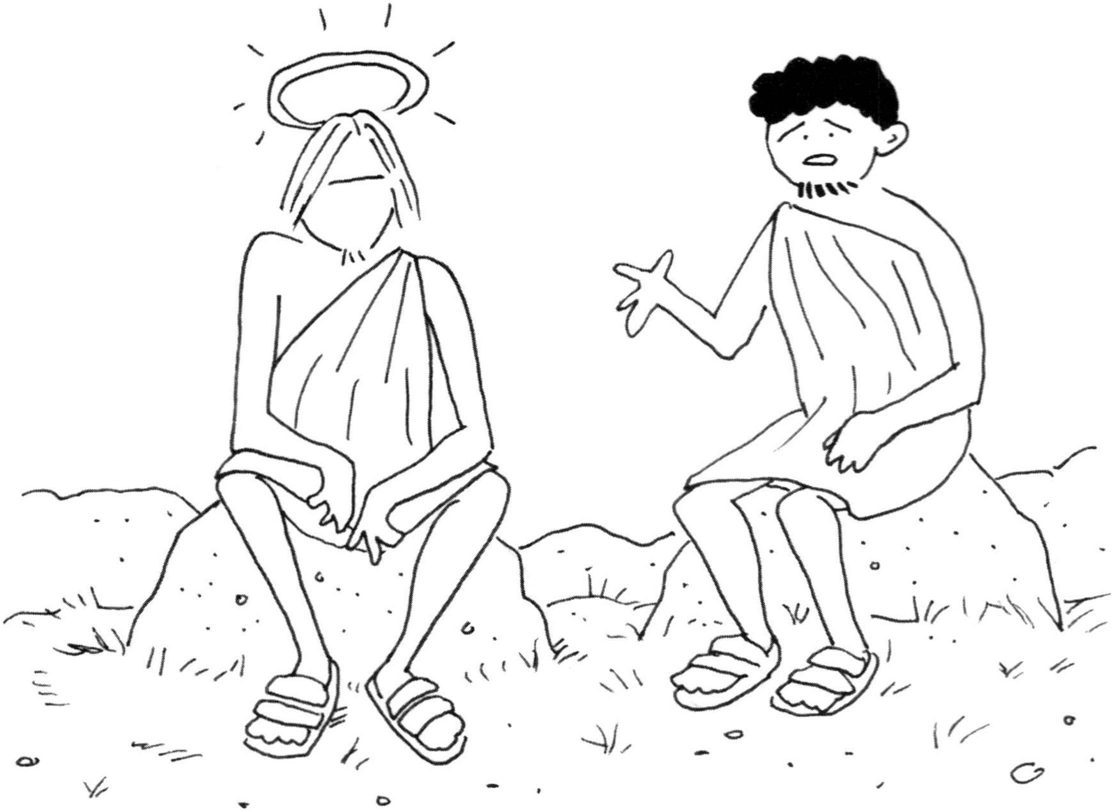

"It's like my father is living vicariously through me.
It's always his dreams, his goals, regardless of what I want.
Ah, but you wouldn't understand, would you, Jesus?"

In the high school talent show, nobody wanted to follow Jesus.

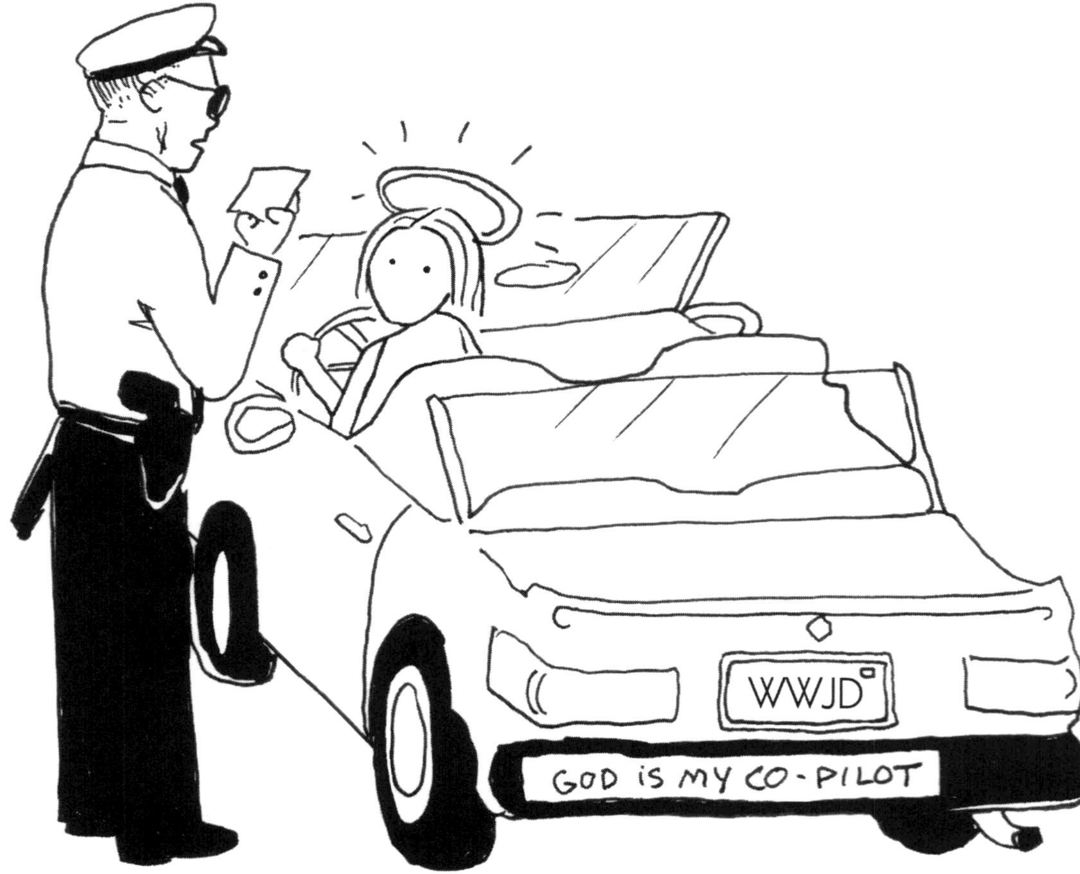
WWJD
GOD IS MY CO-PILOT

"This is only a learner's permit, son. It requires you to have a parent in the vehicle with you at all times."

"All right, boys, you know the drill. Three seconds left, down by one . . . get the ball to Jesus."

"As your guidance counselor, I suggest you rethink your chosen fields. I don't see a future for you in either 'public speaking' or 'saving mankind.'"

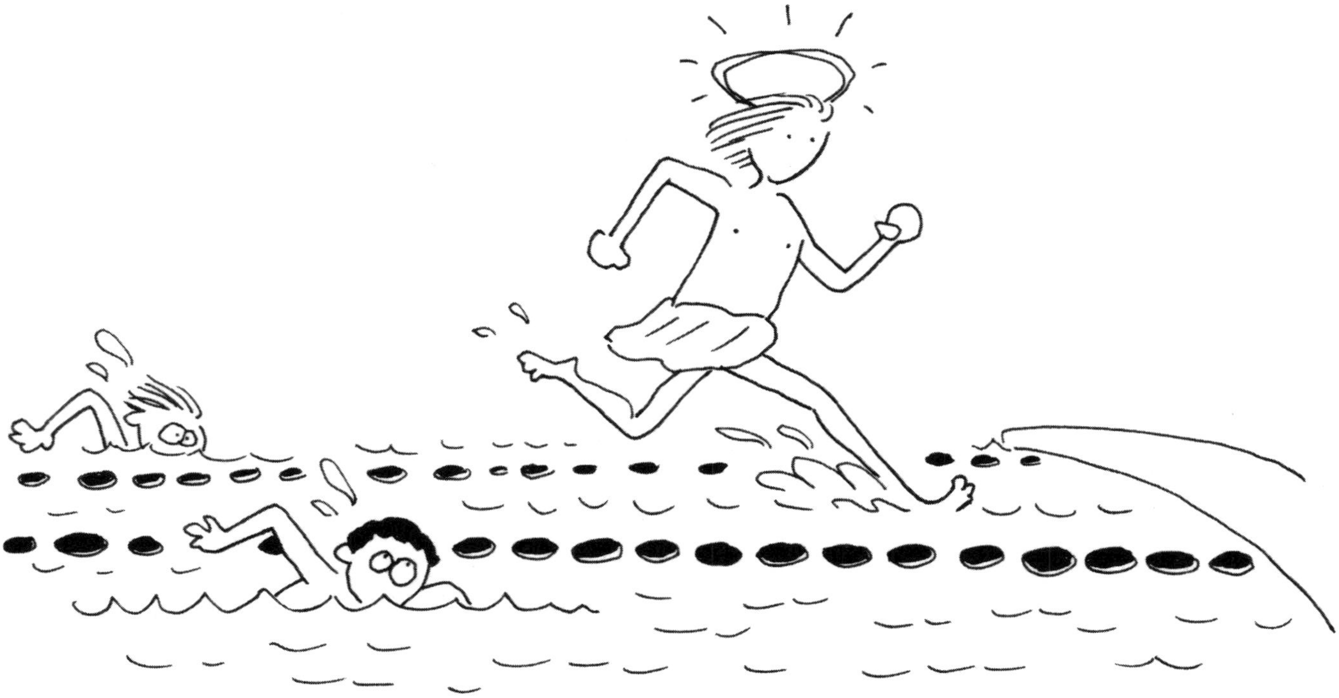

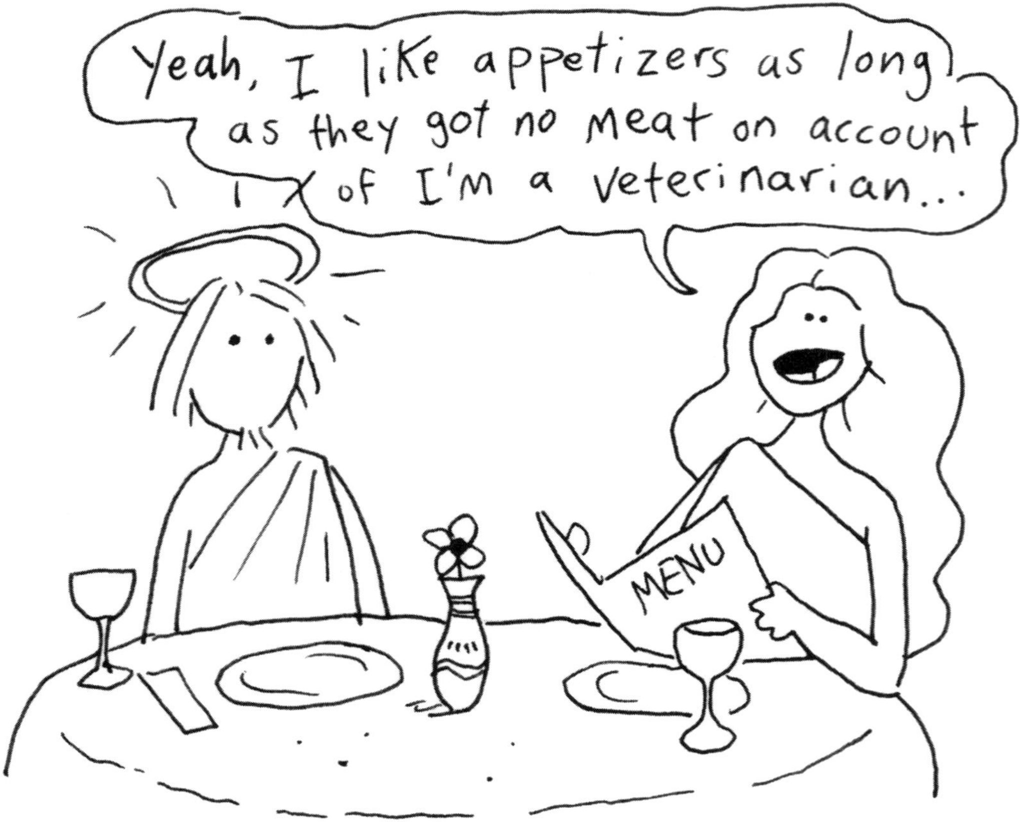
Yeah, I like appetizers as long as they got no meat on account of I'm a veterinarian...
MENU

He could cure the blind, but He couldn't cure the blonde.

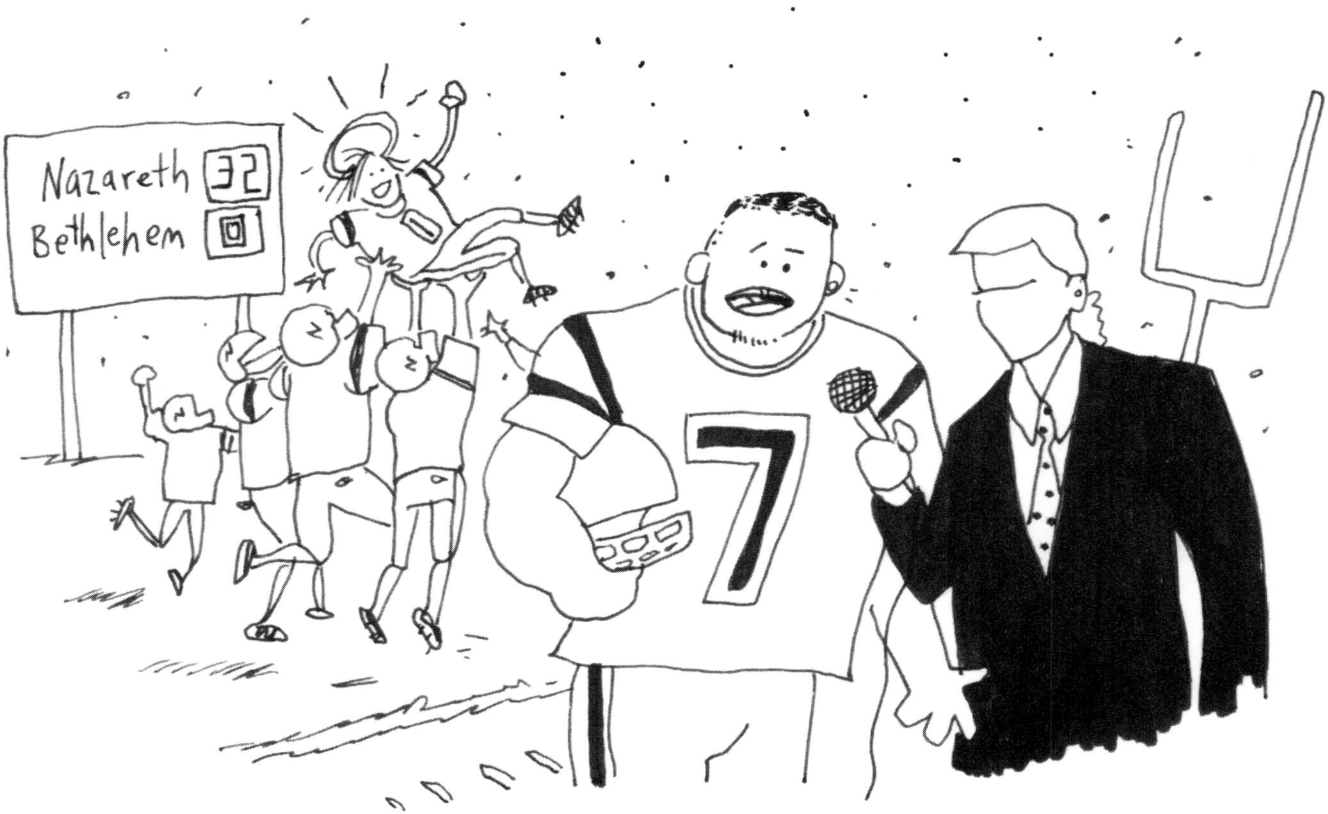
Nazareth 32
Bethlehem 0
7

"It was a great team effort, but we couldn't have won without
the help of our Lord and Savior, Jesus Christ."

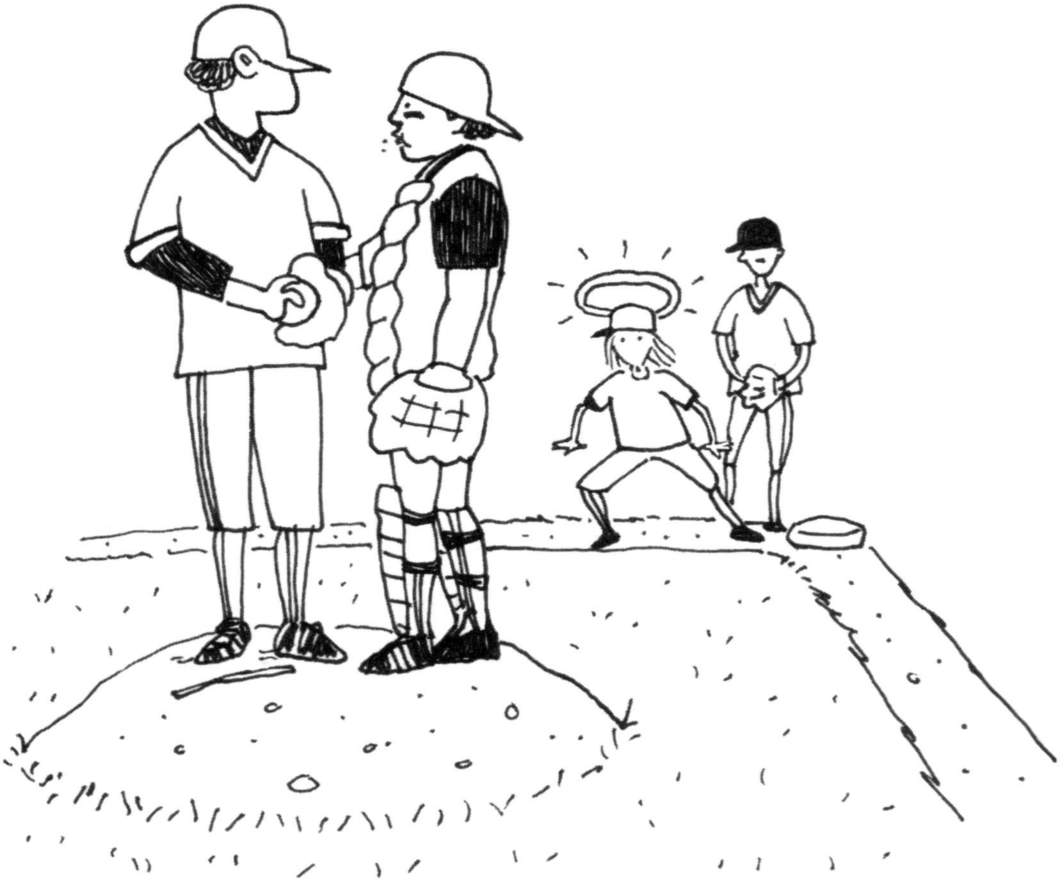

“Don’t worry about the runner . . . He shalt not steal.”

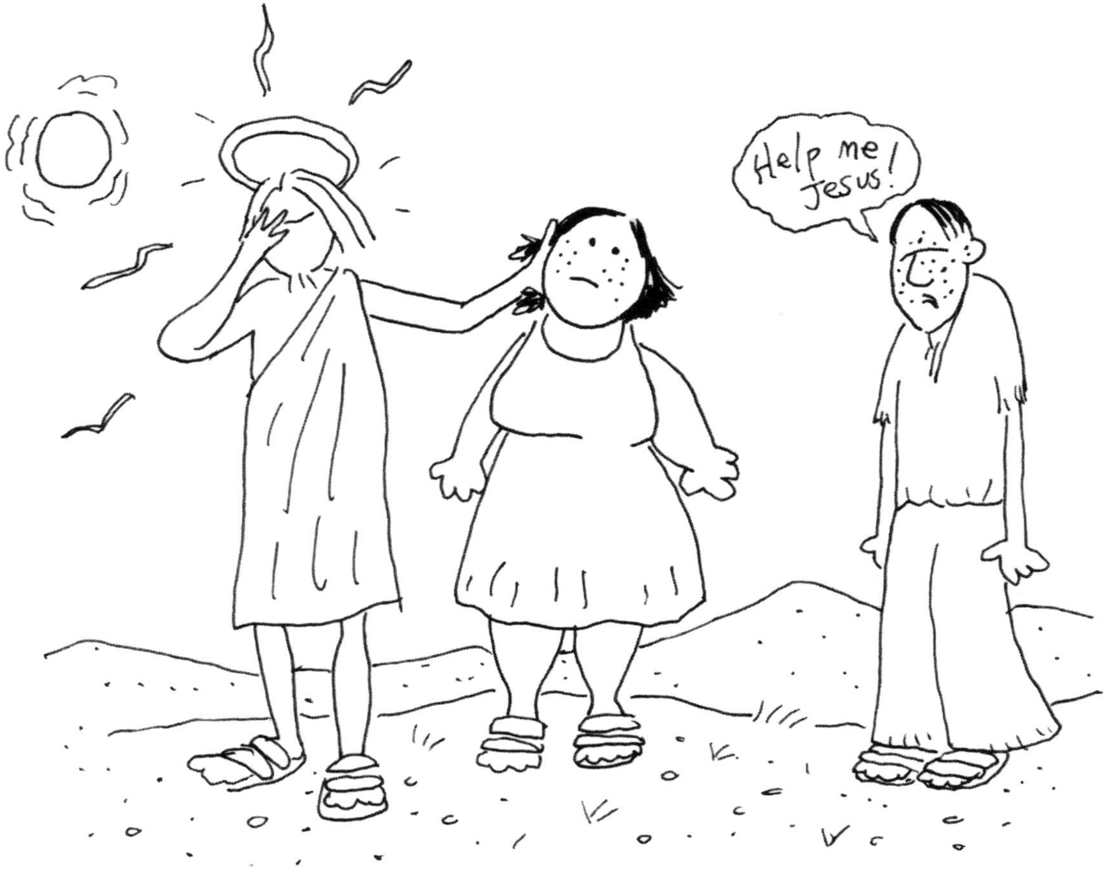
Help me! Jesus!

Lesser-Known Miracle #2: Jesus cures chronic acne in local youth.

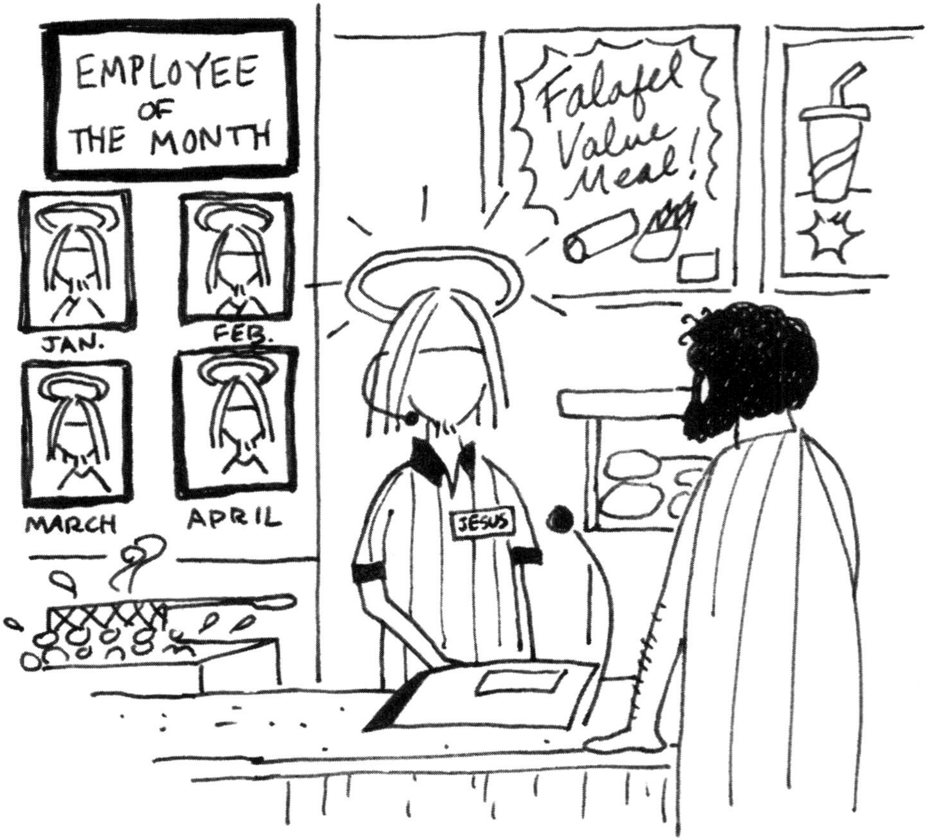
EMPLOYEE OF THE MONTH
JAN.
FEB.
MARCH
APRIL
Falafel Value Meal!
JESUS

Despite his best efforts, Jesus could not create a miracle
when it came to Irvin M. Knucklebaum.

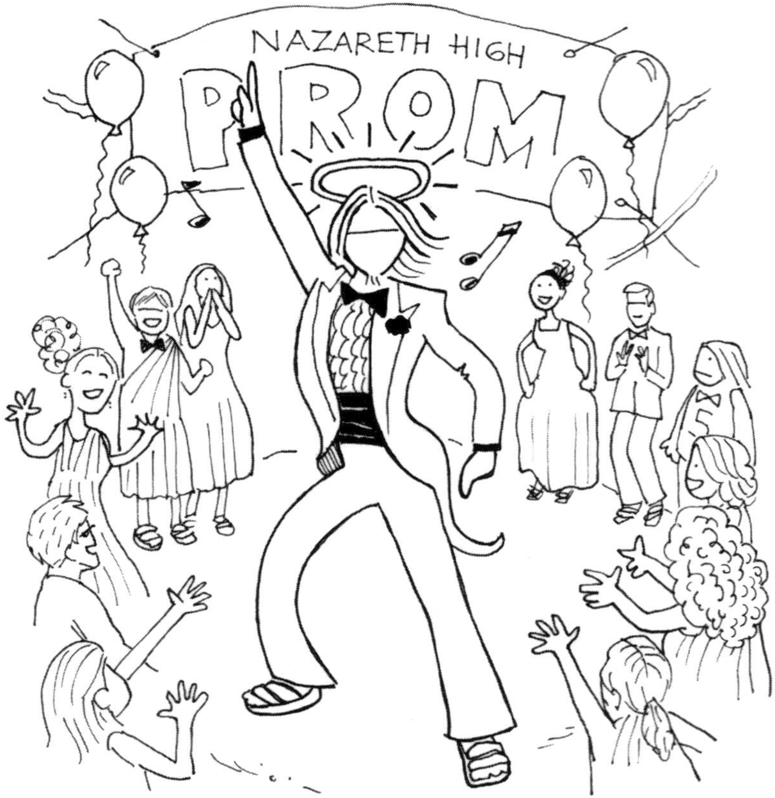
NAZARETH HIGH
PROM

Lord of the Dance

About the Scribes

Spencer Smith and Mark Penta are lifelong friends who met in first grade and attended catechism school together.

Mark draws. Spencer tries to be funny.